CONDUCTING MEANINGFUL EXPERIMENTS

CONDUCTING MEANINGFUL EXPERIMENTS

40 Steps to Becoming a Scientist

R. Barker Bausell

SAGE Publications
International Educational and Professional Publisher
Thousand Oaks London New Delhi

For information address:

 SAGE Publications, Inc.
2455 Teller Road
Thousand Oaks, California 91320

SAGE Publications Ltd.
6 Bonhill Street
London EC2A 4PU
United Kingdom

SAGE Publications India Pvt. Ltd.
M-32 Market
Greater Kailash I
New Delhi 110 048 India

Printed in the United States of America

Library of Congress Cataloging-in-Publication Data

Bausell, R. Barker
    Conducting meaningful experiments : 40 steps to becoming a scientist / R. Barker Bausell.
        p. cm.
    Includes bibliographical references and index.
    ISBN 0-8039-5530-8. — 0-8039-5531-6 (pbk.)
    1. Research—Methodology. 2. Scientists—Vocational guidance.
    I. Title.
Q180.55.M4B38   1994
001.4'34—dc20   93-42140

94 95 96 97 98 10 9 8 7 6 5 4 3 2 1

Sage Production Editor: Astrid Virding

Contents

Introduction

The purpose of this book is to help prospective social, behavioral, and health scientists conduct meaningful research. Meaningfulness can, of course, be conceptualized in a number of ways. I happen to define a meaningful research study as one that has the potential of actually helping people and improving the human condition. Other people would define the term more broadly, such as anything that contributes to theory formation or any research capable of explaining the etiology of a scientifically significant phenomenon.

The truth of the matter is, however, that how one goes about ensuring the meaningfulness of his or her research is far more important than the way the term itself is defined. The very acts of (1) formally considering the potential meaningfulness of one's research prior to conducting it, and (2) taking all of the necessary steps to enhance this potential, will result in better, more meaningful science irrespective of how one defines what is and is not meaningful.

There are a finite number of discrete steps, which, if conscientiously followed, will produce better, more reliable, more meaningful research regardless of whether one believes that the purpose of research in his or her discipline is (1) to improve the human condition, (2) to refine theory, or (3) to achieve any other epistemologically defensible objective. The presentation and explanation of these discrete steps correspondingly comprise the bulk of this book.

Just as opinions differ with respect to the ultimate purpose of social, behavioral, and health research, so too do assessments regarding its cumulative accomplishments. Given my orientation toward searching for individually and/or societally useful findings, I tend to be quite disappointed with our successes so far in producing results that actually have the potential to make a difference in people's lives. I suspect that the same is true for those who value the development of very specific social and behavioral theory, since results that add anything substantive to our understanding of the etiology of important personal, societal, or scientific outcomes also appear to be disconcertingly rare. We have few if any sociological theories, for example, that are capable of predicting the occurrence of new phenomena as Einstein's general theory of relativity was able to do. We have very few psychological findings that are capable of making people happier or more satisfied with their lives. We have very little educational research that teachers can use to help their students learn more during the course of a school day.

Although there is no shortage of opinions, no one knows for sure why this is so. There are at least four possibilities:

1. Too much research is conducted with too little consideration of its social, professional, or scientific implications. This problem is easily ameliorated by the formal evaluation of these implications prior to conducting a study. Chapters 2 through 4 are therefore specifically dedicated to the process of formulating and evaluating important, relevant (i.e., meaningful) research questions.

2. Too much research of dubious quality is being conducted. Since no one ever purposefully sets out to conduct a poor research study, the reason so many flawed efforts find their way into the literature must be due to either a lack of sound empirical principles or a lack of understanding of those that do exist. I personally happen to know that the former is not true, since I recently spent 2 years of my life assimilating what has become a truly enormous literature devoted exclusively to the methodological aspects of conducting empirical research. After reviewing more than 5,000 articles and books, I abstracted 2,660 of these references for the resulting 800+ page volume (Bausell, 1991). *Conducting Meaningful Experiments* is a direct result of this effort, because I have become convinced that this vast, disparate literature can be reduced to a finite number of empirical principles that are capable of enhancing the quality of all our research efforts. The bulk of the present book, then, is devoted to the presentation of a series of generally accepted principles (or "rules") for conducting empirical research capable of producing the types of results that the scientific community as a whole is most likely to accept. I believe that a firm grasp of these principles (especially those presented in Chapters 5 and 6), along with an a priori commitment to quality at the design stage, will greatly enhance the probability that any researcher will ultimately produce valid, methodologically sound work.

3. Too much research is carried out by people who really aren't scientists in any true sense of the word. Becoming a scientist requires specialized training, considerable hands-on experience, and a painstaking acculturation process. To require someone to do research as a condition, say, for being allowed to teach in a university makes no more sense than to require a nonartist to periodically paint a canvas or compose a sonata. I happen to believe that a scientist is motivated almost exclusively by an internal drive, which can perhaps be facilitated, but certainly not externally instilled. The only way of knowing whether one has this type of motivation, however, is to actually start conducting research and see how one likes it. I firmly believe that anyone who truly wants to be a researcher can be a researcher. The concepts involved just aren't that technically or conceptually difficult to master. A major purpose of this book, therefore, is to help make the conduct of one's first research study as meaningful an experience as possible, so that the reader can evaluate whether he or she wants to forge a career in this arena.

4. Too often the ultimate objective of the research process appears to be a discrete "publishable" study rather than a substantive contribution to science or society. Research should not be conducted solely as an item-by-item addition to one's curriculum vitae. Instead, it should be a concentrated search for something, which does not end until a discrete, recognizable discovery is made. This discovery, in turn, almost always seems to point to the need for a new search for a new piece of an ever-evolving puzzle. It is the search process itself, however, that differentiates science from all other forms of human endeavor. It is also the need to be the first person to solve the puzzle at hand that differentiates a researcher from all our other professions. Any science that is driven by these forces inevitably becomes a river of effort without end, indubitably influenced and made possible by what has gone before. In the final analysis, everything in this book is designed to facilitate this type of discovery and, ultimately, the flow of the river itself.

It cannot be said with absolute certainty that these factors are solely responsible for our perceived slow rate of progress in the social, behavioral, and health sciences. What I can absolutely guarantee, however, is that the advice in this book can improve the quality of any beginning researcher's work if that person is willing to take it.

I am also not saying that this advice is the only path to conducting meaningful research. All I am attempting to do in this book is lend a hand to anyone who aspires to take his or her science one step further than it has been before and, in so doing, make a meaningful contribution to society.

Since there is no way of knowing who will end up reading this book, I have made as few assumptions regarding my potential audience as possible. I therefore assume no technical knowledge at all on the part of my readers, nor will I attempt to impart any. What I will do is give the reader a list of principles that, in one form or another, are absolutely essential for conducting meaningful empirical research involving human subjects.

Conducting meaningful scientific research can be an intensively rewarding experience like none other. Why this is so, I am not sure, but I think it is related to the fact that, since science really is a river of effort without end, any true contribution to it bestows a certain measure of immortality. Or perhaps it is simply that, whether we know it or not, we all aspire to do something worthwhile with our lives.

Who "I" Am

I make my living both by conducting and by helping other people conduct research (which means that I am also a research methodologist). I wouldn't consider trading my job for any other in existence. I think doing research is the most exciting, fulfilling, important career anyone can possibly have and I hope to somehow, someday be in a position to provide my children with the opportunity to engage in the same line of work (if they have any interest in doing so).

Whether I am a good scientist is for posterity to decide. I did have the good fortune to be in a position to make several very interesting discoveries very early in my career, and to this day I have never, except with the birth of my two children, experienced anything as moving or as exhilarating as having just produced a new and important piece of knowledge that no one, anywhere, except me, knew.

I should also mention that I have also made some ridiculous blunders. I have probably made every known genre of empirical mistake at least once. I have pursued blind alleys relentlessly—once even conducting a series of 28 studies trying to find something that I later learned just plain didn't exist. None of these things, however, not the mistakes and not the ill-considered studies, ever served to dampen my enthusiasm for the scientific process. If anything I think such misadventures only tend to make the successes sweeter when they come—and they will come to those who are sufficiently determined.

I also had the very rare good fortune of having access to two very excellent mentors. They are Joseph R. Jenkins (now at the University of Washington), who was the best researcher I ever met at formulating important questions and then being able to design studies to answer them; and William B. Moody (now at the University of Delaware), who gave me the opportunity to do as much research as I could handle as long as I could convince him of its meaningfulness.

Unfortunately, mentors such as these are exceedingly rare in the social, behavioral, and health sciences. All too often students are expected to conduct their first research studies with the minimal guidance of a dissertation committee and later, as junior faculty members, to conduct their first program of research with only the memory of this minimal guidance.

I would therefore be remiss if I did not offer the following piece of advice (which I will present in the form of an empirical principle) as an extremely important strategy in the conduct of meaningful research:

▼

Principle 1: **Conduct your first research study under the tutelage of an experienced, principled mentor.**

▼

The best (and perhaps the only) way to learn how to conduct research is to actually do it. An experienced mentor who has your best interests at heart (hence the "principled" qualifier) can greatly facilitate this learning process and can probably accelerate your learning curve several years. Thus you should search for an experienced researcher with whom to collaborate on your beginning efforts. If this is not possible, then at the very least find such a person with whom you can discuss your prospective study and who is available for consultation during its conduct.

The Scientist as Interventionist

I began this chapter by defining meaningful research as research that has the potential of helping someone. The primary type of research that is capable of accomplishing such an active objective is *empirical research in which the scientist personally introduces an intervention of some sort in order to evaluate its effect upon an important societal outcome.* My second piece of formal advice is therefore:

▼

Principle 2: **When conducting empirical research, always attempt to experimentally manipulate your intervention so that you can directly measure its effect(s).**

▼

The reason for this is quite simple. If your ultimate goal is to help people or to improve the human condition, then you must contribute in some meaningful way to introducing a change in the way people are treated or in the way in which our institutions operate. Since you are not a mystic, you will not automatically know that these changes are "good." As a scientist, the only way to learn whether your innovation is worthwhile is to introduce it under controlled, experimental conditions and measure its hypothesized effects.

Experiments of this sort are often called *intervention studies, experimental studies,* or (depending upon their setting and purpose) *clinical trials.* Their successful conduct is predicated upon the existence of (1) well-developed theory, (2) a considerable amount of developmental work dedicated to the construction of both the interventions and the outcome measures by which these interventions are evaluated, and (3) the utilization of an agreed-upon set of procedures that will allow other scientists to place a certain amount of confidence in any results that accrue therefrom.

As such, intervention studies assume a certain degree of maturity within their parent sciences. They also tend to be more difficult to conduct than other types of research, but there is a growing consensus (especially among the nonscientific community) that it is now time for all of the sciences to begin dedicating more of their truly impressive talents to the task of discovering ways in which the environment can be altered to specifically better the human condition. Concomitantly, there is a growing reluctance on the part of funding agencies to continue supporting "preliminary" studies that never seem to quite realize this promise. There is also a growing realization that our society, beset by ever-multiplying social problems and the escalating costs of caring for a population that is rapidly growing older, no longer has pockets deep enough to finance another generation of preliminary studies.

Because of the difficulty inherent in manipulating many social, behavioral, and health-related variables, compromises must occasionally be made in the design of experiments involving them. Sometimes, for example, we must conduct our experiments under relatively contrived laboratory situations, rather than the real-world crucible of everyday practice. Sometimes we must shorten the experimental interval more than we would like. Sometimes we must settle for accessible subject populations rather than the ones in which we are truly interested. Sometimes we must even alter our outcome variables a bit, making them somewhat less veridical in order to demonstrate change in a reasonable time period.

Suppose, for example, that a preventive researcher believed that he or she could develop a genre of positive health messages that would be more effective in eliciting salutary lifestyle practices than the current negatively oriented ones offered in the media. Because it is highly unlikely that our researcher would have the resources to mount a major community-based study to assess the effectiveness of this new approach, it might first be necessary to randomly assign one group of volunteers to be exposed to a battery of the positive messages and compare their intent to adopt sensible preventive behaviors with a randomly assigned group exposed to comparable negative messages.

Certainly such a study, if successful, would need to be replicated, extended, and made more veridical (e.g., by measuring actual behavior 6 months or so after exposure to the two types of health messages), but studies such as this, which do introduce an experimental intervention and evaluate its effect, have more potential for helping us solve the types of problems we are now facing in society than any other genre of research. Furthermore, with a little creativity (and, alas, perhaps a few initial compromises), most of the important variables in the social, behavioral, and health sciences can be studied under experimental conditions.

Analyzing the results of questionnaires or interviews, observing and recording the way people interact with one another in naturalistic settings, or soliciting opinions and attitudes toward this or that topic are appealing research options, but they won't in and of themselves help us educate our children, improve the quality of our lives, or increase our productivity. Research such as this may suggest directions for doing so and, hence, can be useful developmental tools in refining our experimental interventions, but in the final analysis if changes in the way we are doing things (or in the results we are getting) are our objective, it is change that must be implemented and evaluated under the most controlled conditions possible. By convention, this is the type of evidence demanded by the scientific community simply because this is the type of evidence that produces the most reliable causal inferences available to us.

There is another, less pragmatic reason for conducting experiments, however, and that is the fact that *there is nothing more exhilarating for a scientist than to manipulate something in a way that it has never been manipulated before and to be the first person in history to observe the resulting effects.* There is also nothing more satisfying for someone with such a bent than to take his or her science one step further than it has ever been before and, not coincidentally, to be so registered in its annals. This book is therefore designed to show its readers how to take this step.

Other Types of Scientific Studies

By focusing on the conduct of experiments, I do not mean to denigrate other types of scientific endeavors. Some of society's most important variables are basically nonmanipulable in nature, and I certainly do not suggest that such concerns not be the subject of empirical scrutiny.

I happen to believe, however, that the most direct means of accomplishing what the social, behavioral, and health sciences should be all about is through the conduct of experiments. I also believe that, with a little creativity, most variables can be experimentally manipulated in one form or another.

I certainly do not believe that experimentation is the only way to generate important new knowledge. Many scientists are almost exclusively interested in studying existing relationships among variables. They are, in other words, more interested in documenting what *is* than what *could be*. Studies of this sort (which are variously called *descriptive*, *correlational*, *naturalistic*, or *observational* research) have a venerable place in the history of science, and there is always a need for good research, regardless of genre.

I do happen to believe that the conduct of experimental research is an excellent way of embarking upon a meaningful scientific career, however, and that there is certainly no better way to learn the research process thoroughly. *I think it is fair to say, in fact, that a thorough knowledge of the concepts involved in conducting an experiment is a prerequisite to conducting any type of empirical research (and therefore prerequisite to embarking upon any type of meaningful scientific career).*

Over the years I have also become convinced that there is no other type of research that has quite the same potential for producing meaningful results in the way that I have defined them. Again, however, regardless of the type of research a scientist conducts, the basic principles that govern experimental research apply just as forcibly to nonexperimental designs. Thus if you do decide to limit your research efforts to handing out questionnaires, to reviewing existing records, or to interviewing people, your primary purpose as a scientist will still be to (1) understand the nature of phenomena and (2) predict the exact conditions under which they occur. As with evaluating the meaningfulness of a research study, the procedural steps taken in designing and conducting a study are more important than the actual approach ultimately chosen to achieve this quintessential scientific objective. You can, in other words, produce scientifically meaningful results regardless of the type of research you do as long as you it well. All I am attempting to do in this little book, therefore, is show prospective scientists who truly want (or perhaps even need) to try to make a meaningful contribution to their science and their society one way of doing so. It is really for this purpose, and this purpose alone, that the 38 rules that follow are tendered.

Suggested Readings

Although I've tried to make each chapter as self-contained as possible, there are numerous resources for gaining a more in-depth understanding of the topics contained therein. The suggested readings that follow constitute only a smattering of the many, many excellent books and articles available to beginning researchers. For a more extensive (but far from exhaustive) list, see:

Bausell, R. B. (1991). *Advanced research methodology: A guide to resources*. Metuchen, NJ: Scarecrow Press.

This is an annotated guide to 2,660 research design, measurement, and statistical references deemed by its author to be most usable to practicing researchers.

Two books that I think give the clearest description of the excitement inherent in the scientific enterprise are:

Watson, J. D. (1968). *The double helix*. New York: Atheneum.
Although this book does not deal with experimental research as we define it in the social, behavioral, and health sciences, it provides a wonderful insight into the excitement of discovery and the excitement of the chase for being the first to discover something. The "something" in this case happened to be the structure of DNA; and I think that, after reading this book, experienced researchers in our fields cannot help but feel a little envious that we haven't even gotten around to defining what our big quests should be, or how we will recognize them if we find them.

Johanson, D., & Edey, M. (1981). *Lucy*. New York: Simon & Schuster.
Lucy is also about discovery, and while its "chase scenes" may not be quite as exciting as those in *The Double Helix*, it does provide a powerful lesson in the effort and rewards of making sense out of our research findings. Much of this book is given over to demonstrating how powerful and useful theories can be generated by relatively sparse data. By implication, I think it also shows us that without this time-consuming process, our research data is likely to remain nothing more than numbers stored in a computer (or bones stored in a museum).

1

What You Need (and Don't Need) to Be a Scientist

Let us begin by briefly discussing some of the characteristics that one needs (and doesn't need) to be an effective scientist.

What You Absolutely Need

If we assume that you aspire to a lifestyle somewhere above the poverty line, the first thing you will need is a doctorate. There are exceptions to this rule, but they grow more and more rare, hence the following piece of career counseling:

▼

Principle 3: **Obtain an appropriate doctorate, preferably a Ph.D., as quickly as possible.**

▼

The Ph.D. itself is completely irrelevant to the conduct of empirical research. Yours will be a truly exceptional program if it contains as many as three courses that have any direct applicability to the type of research you wind up doing.

Even though a Ph.D. may be nothing more than a union card, however, it is extremely difficult to find employment doing research without one. (You will need this union card to be fairly compensated, and without it, you will not be afforded the same opportunities to conduct meaningful studies.) I would further advise you to be a full-time doctoral student if at all possible, since this will afford you the best opportunity of working directly with a practicing researcher (Principle 1).

Now that I have done my counseling duties, let us concentrate upon those behaviors that are directly relevant to the actual conduct of research itself. I will begin with the most important scientific principle contained in this book:

▼

Principle 4: **Do not contemplate conducting research if you are not prepared to be absolutely, uncompromisingly, unfashionably honest.**

▼

This is absolutely the most important attribute for a scientist to have. Scientific progress itself is directly dependent upon the integrity of its practitioners. I am not only talking about the avoidance of complete fabrications here, such as painting skin grafts on mice or reporting the results of identical twin studies for children that were never born. I am also referring to the avoidance of small untruths or sins of omission, such as not mentioning seemingly minor things that may have gone wrong during the course of an experiment, in order to enhance its subsequent chances of getting published.

A researcher needs to have the courage to tell the entire truth even if it means effectively throwing away a considerable amount of personal work, delaying graduation, or not obtaining a much-coveted promotion. For those who do not possess this particular characteristic, I personally beg of them to seek another career. Go into public relations or corporate communications. Make twice the salary and drive a Lexus, but please do not go into research. If you do, you will hinder other people's progress and you will ultimately be very dissatisfied with your choice of career.

▼

Principle 5: Do not contemplate conducting research if you are not prepared to work very hard.

▼

Conducting research is an extremely time-consuming enterprise yet, paradoxically, few social, behavioral, or health scientists can pursue it full-time (which might be another reason for our mediocre track record). The pursuit of scientific knowledge is also a process that has no end point, so if you plan to seriously pursue a scientific career, you must be willing to devote many, many long and late hours to your research.

All the successful scientists I have known have had a very high energy level. Whether this is under an individual's control depends upon a number of factors, but I have found the capacity to do research to be similar to the capacity to engage in physical exercise: The more you do, the more you can do, and the more you are willing to do.

Because of this need for continual, concentrated effort, research is, in many ways, a young person's profession. It is far easier to devote the time, energy, and passion it demands prior to taking on, say, familial or administrative responsibilities.

There are exceptions to every generalization of course, but the simple truth is: The more focused and even fanatical a researcher is, the better and more impressive his or her ultimate accomplishments are likely to be. (I personally happen to know that some of the stereotypes in this regard are true, once having helped a MacArthur fellow with a methodological problem who had no residence at all outside of his laboratory.)

The only real way I know around this omnipresent time constraint is to learn to work very fast and to concentrate very hard. I have personally learned to do this over the years, yet every step of the research process always takes more time than I think it will. I still sometimes reanalyze my data again and again—exploring alternative hypotheses, statistically controlling different variables, and looking for implausible interactive or confounding factors that could potentially influence my conclusions. I still sometimes ponder the meaning of my findings for long hours and often go back to the library for one last time-consuming search through a related literature for insights into the problem at hand. Even though I remain able to devote this extra time, however, and even though there is no question that I am technically far more skilled now, I don't think my current work is as exciting or as important as that which I produced as a young man. Perhaps the reason for this is that I no longer bring a young person's passion to my research. Perhaps my research now has too many other competitors. Perhaps this perception isn't even true, so I will abstain from elevating the importance of youth too highly in the scientific process, although I nevertheless advise all aspiring researchers to stay "forever young" as long as they can.

Unfortunately, even hard work is not enough in and of itself. The conduct of meaningful research involves a great deal of preparation, the first step of which is implied by our sixth principle:

Principle 6: **Do not contemplate conducting research until you have mastered your general field or discipline.**

▼

Research is not performed in a vacuum. Knowing how to conduct research is not even enough. Researchers must understand their fields as well as the basic paradigms operating therein. Otherwise, I think they have practically no chance at all of making (or even recognizing) a significant contribution thereto.

Thus, if you are not thoroughly familiar with a field, you should not attempt to conduct research in it. If there isn't any discipline with which you are thoroughly familiar in the academic sense, then you shouldn't conduct research at all. (Unfortunately, I can't give any particularly innovative advice about how to learn a discipline, other than the tried-and-true steps of enrolling in a good graduate program, taking good courses, and studying good textbooks.)

It is true that some people do seem to have an "inborn feel" for what is and is not important in a discipline, but it has been my experience that these individuals also tend to be both knowledgeable about the basic content of their fields and extremely familiar with its research literature. It is my opinion, in fact, that the greatest part of this feel is comprised of very careful attention to two distinct behaviors that will be discussed in detail shortly: reviewing the literature and critically addressing the "So what?" question.

Before considering these two behaviors, however, I would like to offer a complementary stricture to the previous principle that is primarily applicable to applied research (which encompasses a large proportion of the empirical work done in the social, behavioral, and health sciences):

▼

Principle 7: **Do not contemplate conducting applied research (i.e., research whose primary purpose is to change the way people practice their professions) if you are not a practitioner in the area, or if you do not have a co-investigator who is. (Always remember, however, that when you are conducting research, you are first and foremost a researcher.)**

▼

To put it into more concrete terms, one should not conduct research that attempts to improve teaching practices within the schooling paradigm if one is not thoroughly familiar with both teaching and schools. One shouldn't attempt to come up with improved therapeutic practices if one hasn't conducted therapy or isn't thoroughly familiar with the therapeutic process. This isn't to say that you can't conduct learning or therapeutic research if you haven't had direct experience in one of the two areas, *but if the goal of your research is to influence practice, it is absolutely imperative that you have enough direct, hands-on experience to be able to judge what is practical and what is not.* Otherwise, it is just too easy to overlook something that is capable of completely invalidating the potential applicability of whatever treatment or intervention you happen to be investigating. Specific clinical practices, regardless of the discipline, are affected by so many constraints (e.g., costs, staffing/time considerations, and political/ethical issues) that any study that fails to appreciate, address, or at the very least recognize all of them is usually a complete waste of time. It is therefore essential for investigators who want to conduct applied research to either do so in an area in which they have had sufficient applied experience or collaborate with someone who both has this type of experience and has had some research experience. (This latter condition is necessary since an awareness of the built-in constraints of the research process itself is as important as an awareness of those inherent within the clinical process.)

There is another side to this coin, however, and that is reflected by the fact that sometimes one's clinical role/training may seem to conflict with what one must do as a researcher. Clinicians in the helping professions have a very understandable (and laudatory) tendency to want to help people. Experimental researchers, on the other hand, usually hope that half of their subjects will be helped more than the other half. What does a good clinician do, for example, if he or she sees that someone in the control group does need more help? Or that the intervention does appear to be working and that everyone in the control group is automatically disadvantaged?

The answer is that when you are doing research, you must act primarily as a researcher and see your experimental protocol through to its completion. Obviously, if anyone in your study is in need of medical or psychological help, you should immediately refer that subject somewhere that he or she can get the help needed. (Emergency contingencies such as this should always be built into one's protocol anyway.) For nonemergency situations, however, you must remember that as a researcher, your primary duty to your subjects (and your profession) is to run the cleanest possible study, not to deliver care.

By the same token, as a researcher you have just as much obligation to protect your subjects as any clinician ever has for his or her patients. You must, in other, words:

1. Never physically endanger your research subjects in any way.
2. Never subject them to any sort of emotional or psychological distress.
3. Never embarrass them in any way (if this is part of the experimental intervention, choose another line of research).
4. Always protect their dignity and freedom of choice (including the freedom to leave your study at any time of their own choosing, regardless of reason).
5. Always treat them as you would wish to be treated (or as you would wish your children or your aging parents to be treated).

What You Should Have (but May Not Absolutely Need) to Be a Researcher

There are a number of attributes, which, while important, probably do not deserve the status of principles. Among these are:

1. You should be driven. This goes a bit further than Principle 5. To call someone "driven" is not particularly complementary in this society, but all those I have ever known who have been extremely successful in their areas of endeavor have possessed this characteristic. I used to be a serious weight lifter, for example, and all the very best lifters that I knew (whether Olympic lifters, bodybuilders, or power lifers) pursued their training with a single-minded intensity that subordinated everything else in their lives. I'm sure that this struck their non-weight-lifting acquaintances as patently absurd, but there is really no other way to excel at something, science included. The correlates of this particular characteristic may be too high a price for many people to pay, but this is a personal choice.

Intensity of purpose may be sufficient anyway. By this I mean a mind-set that ensures that the study under consideration is always being thought about, always being mentally played over and over, and always being examined for possible flaws and extensions. If enough intensity can be brought to the task at hand, to ensure that nothing that needs to be done on *this* study is postponed or delayed, then I think it should be possible to fashion a rewarding study-by-study career without sacrificing any other truly important aspects of life (except possibly either some leisure time or some sleep).

2. You should have a certain amount of innate curiosity. Some of the motivation to be hardworking and driven comes from the external rewards available to researchers. Scientists, especially later in their careers, probably like money and professional advancement as well as does anyone else. In general, however, science is not as good a choice as investment banking, medicine, or plumbing for someone for whom the material things in life are of utmost importance.

What scientists usually treasure more is their status among their colleagues and the opportunity to receive credit for their accomplishments. In the long run, however, it is probably even more important for a scientist to have a basic need to know the answer to the questions at hand *and a need to be the first person in the history of the human race to solve a particular puzzle or problem.* It is this need, drive, or compulsion that truly motivates scientists, especially young ones, to make the sacrifices necessary to excel at their task. The presence of such drives, in fact, makes doing what has to be done really no sacrifice at all, especially after the first true success is achieved. One of the primary services that I am attempting to offer by writing this book, therefore, is simply to increase the speed with which this initial success comes.

3. You should be skeptical. It is important for a researcher not to take things at face value, because a large part of science entails questioning obvious truths that other people take for granted. Good researchers see the need to confirm or disconfirm generalizations, everyday common-sense statements, and other bromides that their peers accept without question.

Good scientists also tend to have specially honed antennae for such lead-ins as "experts say" or "research says" or "the literature says" or "everybody knows." One of my most influential experiences as a beginning graduate student came when the instructor, a leading Piaget scholar of the time, asked each student in a doctoral seminar why Piagetian theory was important to his or her particular area of concentration. Mine happened to be mathematics education at the time, so I used a time-honored opening for seasoned students who know the importance of giving instructors what they want to hear by saying something like: "Well, obviously Piaget is relevant to mathematics education because . . . " at which point the researcher interrupted me and said, "It's not obvious to me."

I was so shocked by this that I simply admitted ignorance to the answer and found the experience so refreshing that I have freely admitted ignorance or skepticism in similar situations ever since. In other words, *I gave up intellectual bullshitting and, equally important, stopped accepting it from other people.* This, I think, is a vital attribute for a researcher to develop and perhaps is really subsumed under the fourth principle (i.e., being "absolutely, uncompromisingly, unfashionably honest").

4. You should be methodical. Conducting a research study is comprised of a number of often tedious, discrete behaviors, any one of which—if improperly performed—can torpedo the entire effort. What this means, then, is that *a researcher needs to have the patience to check and recheck each step performed, as well as to rethink every decision made.* This can be especially difficult when one possesses a great deal of curiosity and is driven to work fast, but please be assured of its importance by one who has been reminded of the veracity of this particular lesson the hard way (and probably still hasn't completely mastered it).

5. You should be open-minded. I would like to emphasize the "should" here, because being open-minded isn't a particularly pervasive scientific virtue. Researchers tend to inexorably belong to a given school of thought (or paradigm), which in turn tends to color and mold both the questions they ask and the interpretations they bring to the data they use to answer them. In many ways this is beneficial, because paradigms or theories can be quite useful in generating interesting, meaningful hypotheses. It can be equally disadvantageous, however, because these same constructions can blind researchers to alternative interpretations of their data. (Researchers subscribing to two opposing theories often can and do view the same results as categorically confirming their worldviews.)

I know of no cure for this state of affairs other than to aspire to a certain degree of humility (which definitely doesn't tend to be a common scientific virtue). This in turn will allow you to at least consider the possibility that you can be wrong when you attempt to interpret the meaning or implications of your findings. If the history of science tells us anything, it is that if you become a scientist, you will ultimately be proved wrong in how you view things—if your research is important enough to motivate anyone to bother to disconfirm it. In science it is not imitation that is the sincerest form of flattery, but rather generating enough interest in your work to have it extended, improved upon, and possibly even attacked.

There are other helpful scientific attributes, but the ones I have mentioned here seem to me to be the most important. Before going on to other things, however, I would like to mention a couple that I really did not forget to list:

1. You don't need to have any real mathematical ability. A lot of people avoid conducting research because they never really understood trigonometry and were afraid to even tackle calculus. With the advent of extremely easy-to-use computerized statistical packages, however, such mathematical skills are no longer necessary in any of the sciences involving human subjects. It does help to be able to estimate grossly what one's results should look like, but even this isn't necessary if you are critical (and methodical) enough to question the computer output and to check and recheck each step in the research process.

2. You don't have to be a genius. Geniuses are rare. Being gifted isn't even as big an advantage in conducting an empirical research study as you would think. Being methodical, determined, and willing to work hard more than makes up for any lack of giftedness. This book is, after all, titled "Conducting Meaningful Experiments," not "How to Formulate an Alternative to the Theory of Relativity." To accomplish the latter, or to stimulate a paradigmatic shift, you do need to be a genius (and you will definitely need someone a lot smarter than I to advise you).

Suggested Readings

There are a number of books written on what it takes to be a scientist and what good scientists should and should not do. Here I will list only one example of what I consider to make the most interesting reading from each of the topics covered in Chapter 1.

Committee on the Conduct of Science of the National Academy of Sciences. (1989). *On being a scientist*. Washington, DC: National Academy Press.

> This is a brief (14 pp.) report, prepared as an introduction to the scientific process, aimed at students contemplating careers as scientists. It is clearly written and emphasizes, among other things, the subjective nature of the scientific enterprise as well as its more important mores (e.g., honesty).

Kohn, A. (1988). *False prophets*. New York: Basil Blackwell.

> This well-written book covers dozens of cases of scientific fraud, both classic and modern, and contains just about everything anyone would ever need to know about the topic. Its 412 references also constitute the most thorough bibliography of which I am aware.

Medawar, P. B. (1979). *Advice to a young scientist*. New York: Harper & Row.

> This is a charming little book, written by an eminent British scientist, that covers not only "advice" to young scientists but also some of the things that are good and bad about the research process.

Mahoney, M. J. (1976). *Scientists as subject: The psychological imperative*. Cambridge, MA: Ballinger.

> This is an iconoclastic look at scientists (who the author sees as "probably the most passionate of professionals") from one psychologist's viewpoint. There is no way of knowing whether the author is right in his conclusions, but the book does provide interesting food for thought for anyone specifically interested in this particular topic.

2

Laying the Foundation

The First Step

As Yogi Berra should have said, "You can't begin until you begin." Had he said this, and had he been a researcher, it would have been translatable to: "The only way to become a scientist is to begin to conduct research." This chapter is dedicated to the preliminary groundwork needed for this beginning.

▼

Principle 8: **Know the relevant research literature thoroughly.**

▼

There is no question that this is the single rule most often violated by beginning researchers. It is very typical for a student or recent doctorate, faced with the need or desire to conduct a research study, to begin the research process in the following manner:

1. A general idea concerning the research question/topic is formulated by brainstorming, with or without some colleagues.
2. A cursory literature review (often consisting of a computerized search) is then undertaken to make sure that the study hasn't

already been "done." (Occasionally this second step will precede the first, which is certainly preferable.)

3. The research question is narrowed down into a testable hypothesis, and the study is begun. (Occasionally, this third step will precede the second, which is certainly not preferable.)

Although I have personally been guilty of performing a study in something approaching this sequence, I have never conducted any meaningful work in this way and I seriously doubt whether anyone else has either. It is my firm opinion, in fact, that a thorough knowledge of the relevant research literature is the most important precursor to formulating an important, meaningful hypothesis.

The literature review, which is the process by which this prerequisite knowledge is achieved, is such an integral step in the research process that most serious, experienced researchers probably don't even consider it a step at all. Instead, they constantly keep abreast of the research taking place in their areas by reading the primary journals and attending research conferences. They are often even aware of important results before they are published via personal communication with similarly minded colleagues.

Without beating this point to death, then, allow me to list a number of reasons why you should acquire a thorough knowledge of the research literature in your area prior to conducting a study.

1. If you have a study in mind, you will find out whether it has already been performed.
2. Regardless of whether you already have a study in mind, you will obtain ideas for hypotheses in need of testing. These ideas can come from:
   a. theoretical and conceptual articles or books that predict what types of interventions are most likely to work in a given field, as well as ideas concerning the determinants of important outcome variables therein,
   b. actual suggestions regarding needed research tendered by other investigators in the discussion sections of their research articles,
   c. an already completed study that you think needs to be redone (e.g., because of a methodological glitch or because it was non-experimental in nature to begin with), or

    d. a good study that needs to be extended (e.g., by improving upon its intervention, substituting a different outcome variable, or even extrapolating it to a different field involving a completely different population).

3. You will see how other, more experienced researchers measured and/or manipulated the variables in which you are interested. In relation to this, you may obtain some very useful procedural ideas for conducting the studies (e.g., types and numbers of subjects to use).

4. Once you do begin to formulate a testable hypothesis, you may be able to ascertain how likely you are to get the results you hope to obtain, which is important, given the difficulty often encountered in publishing null results.

Since most beginning researchers have not been continually monitoring the research going on in their area for any length of time, Principle 8 must be accomplished by a discrete set of behaviors called "the literature review." Because of the importance of this process, I will offer the following relatively negative piece of advice prior to discussing some of the more positive behaviors involved therein:

▼

Principle 9: **When conducting a literature review, do not rely exclusively on computerized literature searches, on abstracting services, on the literature in a single discipline, or on an arbitrarily defined time period.**

▼

Although they produce woefully incomplete results, computerized literature search and/or abstracting services do have considerable potential as starting points. Some of the databases most commonly used by social and behavior scientists therefore follow:

Applied Social Sciences Index and Abstracts
Arts and Humanities Citation Index
Biological Abstracts

Books in Print
British Books in Print
British Education Index
Canadian Education Index

Child Abuse & Neglect
Child Development Abstracts and
　　Bibliography
Computer and Control Abstracts
Computer and Information Systems
　　Abstracts Journal
Criminal Justice Periodical Index
Current Contents (Social & Behavioral
　　Sciences)
Current Index to Journals in Education
Current Index to Statistics: Applica-
　　tions, Methods, and Theory
Current Technology Index
CRISP: National Institute of Mental
　　Health
Dissertation Abstracts International
Educational Administration Abstracts
Education Index
Exceptional Child Education Resources
Excerpta Medica
Family Resources
Federal Research in Progress
Government Reports Announcements
　　& Index
Higher Education Abstracts
Human Resources Abstracts
Index of Economic Articles
Index Medicus
Interagency Panel Information System
International Bibliography of Politi-
　　cal Science
International Political Science
　　Abstracts
Journal of Economic Literature
Library of Congress Catalog

Linguistics and Language Behavior
　　Abstracts
Medical Literature and Retrieval
　　System
Mental Health Abstracts
National Clearinghouse for Mental
　　Health Information
National Criminal Justice Reference
　　Service
National Institute for Mental Health
　　Grants and Contracts Informa-
　　tion System
National Technical Information Service
PAIS International (Public Affairs
　　Information Service)
Psychological Abstracts
PsycSCAN
Research Abstracts
Research in Education
Research Into Higher Education
　　Abstracts
Sage Race Relations Abstracts
Sage Urban Studies Abstracts
Science Citation Index
Smithsonian Science Information
　　Exchange
Social Sciences Citation Index
Social Work Research & Abstracts
Sociological Abstracts
Sociology of Education Abstracts
Statistical Theory and Method
　　Abstracts
U.S. Government Printing Office
　　Publications
U.S. Political Science Documents

The Literature Review

To see what is entailed in finding the relevant literature surrounding a given topic, let us assume an almost zero starting point. Specifically, let us assume that you have a few general textbooks touching the topic at hand, a couple of slightly more focused journal articles, and a preliminary computerized literature review from one or more of the relevant available databases.

Given such a beginning point, I would suggest the following steps:

1. Decide exactly what it is you are searching for and how widely you are willing to stray. If your goal is to find specific studies involving one or more specific variables, then articulate what these are at the onset.

2. Solicit some help from someone who has either conducted research in the area or who teaches therein. Things that might be reasonable to ask of such an individual are:

  a. to be allowed to photocopy any bibliographies available,
  b. the location of any narrative literature reviews or meta-analyses of the area in which you are interested (such documents will allow you to "hit the ground running" by typically supplying more than 100 references, plus at least one person's opinion regarding what they all "mean"),
  c. what journals are the most likely to contain relevant research articles,
  d. the name of someone else that you might approach, and
  e. the names of any seminal studies and/or books on the topic.

In return, you might promise to share a copy of any interesting sources that you uncover. Doctoral dissertations (which are abstracted by topic area in *Dissertations International*) constitute an especially good source of reference lists (actually their literature reviews are often their strongest component).

3. Check the reference lists of the sources with which you started with any obtained via the second step. Look up any sources whose titles sound promising. Skim them for relevance (you can often ascertain this via the study's abstract and/or procedures section) and read the promising ones carefully. Next, go through these new reference lists in the same way. Keep track of any relevant articles obtained by filing them alphabetically in folders and by entering them in a word processing file (see Principle 10) accompanied by your own abstracts.

4. Once you have a feel for the journals that tend to publish the type of articles you are looking for, carefully go through the year-end title indices (which are usually presented in the last issue of each volume), beginning with the most recently bound volume and preceding backward in time. Continue this until it's obvious that you aren't going to find anything else of interest. When you have completed this process, repeat Step 3, above, with any new articles, being on the lookout for additional relevant journals. Also be on the lookout for published literature reviews and meta- analyses since they are especially valuable sources of individual research studies. (A few journals are completely given over to these summations, such as *Review of Educational Research, Psychological Bulletin,* and the *Annual Review* journals that cover a number of discrete disciplines.) Edited books are especially good sources of chapters devoted to theoretical and conceptual overviews based upon extensive literature reviews surrounding a particular topic. There is also at least one major publisher (Greenwood Press located in Westport, Connecticut) that specializes in bibliographies, both of information sources and of discrete, often quite esoteric research literatures.

5. Solicit the help of one of your university's reference librarians. Often this won't be particularly fruitful, but they might be able to steer you toward a reference book or a helpful bibliography with which you are unfamiliar. (Actually, an interesting use of an hour or so of leisure time is to systematically peruse the volumes housed in the reference section of a major research library. The wealth of information contained there is quite amazing.)

6. Consult the Social Science Citation Index *(or its physical science counterpart).* Although recommended only for the conscientious (who also have good eyesight), these volumes allow the user to find sources that have cited an earlier study which you have ascertained to be especially relevant to the purposes at hand, which of course gives the new study a high probability of being relevant as well. (Most libraries now offer these services on-line.)

7. Check your expanded reference list against your original computerized literature search. For those relevant studies contained in the former but not the latter, find out if they are contained in the databases you searched. If they are, check the keywords under which they are indexed and redo your search, using those words. If the additional references are not listed in the searched databases, find out where they are listed (see the sources above) and search them.

8. Although this step is usually not necessary, leaders in the field in which you are interested could be contacted and asked to suggest additions to your current bibliography. This could consist of simply mailing your bibliography to promising names (journal articles typically provide their authors' addresses), along with a stamped, self-addressed return envelope, asking for additions thereto. (It will be helpful if you provide a sentence or two describing the exact purpose of your bibliography.) For every five you send out you might receive one back with a couple of new references.

9. Once you have completed what is really a major undertaking, continually update it by monitoring the primary journals (and conference proceedings) devoted to the line of research in which your are interested.

Obviously, this combination of manual and electronic processes is extremely time-consuming, and the nonautomated steps are judged by many people to be quite old-fashioned. Personally, I think that there are no real options open to the truly serious researcher. Experienced researchers have always accumulated their research literature manually by prospectively monitoring relevant journals over time and keeping in contact with other researchers in their fields, so what I am suggesting is not as reactionary as it may seem. Furthermore, once completed, such a reference list can be updated with a minimum of effort and used for a variety of purposes (including Principle 10, below).

▼

Principle 10: **Learn to use a major word-processing program and utilize it to produce an annotated bibliography based upon your literature review.**

▼

Just about every step of the research process can be greatly facilitated via the use of a personal computer, especially if you learn to compose directly on the keyboard rather than on paper. (Writing an annotated bibliography is an excellent way to do this, since polished prose is not a particularly high priority.) Thus, if you don't know how to use a widely employed word-processing program such as *WordPerfect*, take the time to learn how to do so prior to beginning your literature review. The time benefits are truly staggering. As an extreme example, my annotated bibliography mentioned earlier contained more than 4,000 names, which had to be alphabetized for the book's author index. My personal computer did this for me in about 30 seconds. It is difficult to imagine how long this would have taken if done manually, but I estimate that it would have necessitated a stack of index cards almost 4 feet high.

The best way to learn the use of a word-processing program is to begin with a specific task (such as the compilation of an annotated bibliography) and secure the help of a hands-on tutor to help you get started. Although I own no stock in the company, I would suggest *WordPerfect* because it is so widely used. (This makes it easier to secure the help of a tutor and it also helps ensure that what you produce is more likely to be transferable to a professional secretary's work station.) Whatever software package you select, you will probably be better off learning the latest version, even though most companies seem to come out with a complete update every 2 weeks to protect their cash flow.

If the services of a tutor are not available (and I would definitely suggest it would be cost-effective to pay one out-of-pocket if a volunteer cannot be had), then the next best strategy is to obtain an easy-to-follow book on the use of the word-processing program you select. (Most company software manuals are written either by someone for whom English is a third language or by certifiable sadists.) Personally, I have always found books published by the Que Corporation to be quite clearly written.

Regardless of the method by which you produce your annotated bibliography, I strongly suggest you take one further step with this document:

Principle 11: **Take the time to write a review article and conduct a meta-analysis based upon the references you have amassed.**

▼

This may seem like an imposing task, but it is absolutely essential that you thoroughly assimilate the information you have collected. There is no better way to do this than by writing an article based upon it. (It is also important to assimilate this literature while the articles that you have read are still fresh in your mind and while it is still feasible to alter your design, based upon the strategies previous researchers in the area have used.)

You may not wind up publishing the resulting paper, but you should definitely proceed on the assumption that you will. What you should try to do, then, is make sense out of the overall gestalt that reading the articles in question has produced. Do not, in other words, write what amounts to a prose connection for a list of references such as: "Jones (1986), Smith (1990), and Wiley (1980) have conducted research involving manipulation of xxx, while Johnson (1987), Nash (1988), and Wrangly et al. (1992) have studied correlates thereof."

Instead, I suggest that you:

1. Describe the important studies briefly.
2. Don't be afraid to criticize them if you think they contain flaws.
3. Don't be afraid to go out on a limb in order to summarize whatever conclusions you think can be safely made based upon them, and most important.
4. Always keep the study you are planning in mind and review all previous research within that framework, for it is at this point that you are most likely to come up with a meaningful hypothesis to test.

Finally, once you are sure that you have located all the relevant studies in your area of interest, I would suggest that you take the time to compute an average effect size for the relationship or difference that you are interested in. (For simple experiments, an effect size is nothing more than the difference between the experimental and control group means divided by the control group's standard deviation.) Called meta-analysis, this is an especially valuable technique for estimating how many subjects you should employ in your actual study (Principle 28). It is also not a particularly difficult task once the relevant literature has been located, read, and abstracted. If a meta-analysis has already been conducted in the area, then I would suggest that you update it by computing an average effect size for the studies that have been completed since its publication. (See the Suggested Readings section for references dealing with the conduct of a meta-analysis.)

Conceptualizing Your Intervention
and Outcome Variables

In truth, the primary purpose of all of the steps suggested in this chapter is to facilitate the formulation of a meaningful hypothesis. It is hoped you will therefore have read and abstracted each article that you have found within this framework. If you have, you should now be in a position to select what may be the single most important component of such a hypothesis: the experimental outcome that your study is designed to influence. The next logical step in our quest is therefore to:

Principle 12: **Select an important, meaningful outcome variable that directly reflects a discrete societal or individual good.**

Although the latter part of this dictum may seem a bit restrictive, I think it is quite reasonable, given the purposes of the social, behavioral, and health sciences. (I would personally go even further in this regard and define a meaningful outcome as one that is directly related to someone's quality of life.) This relatively narrow definition certainly reduces the range of reasonable outcome variables available to researchers; but in many ways this is more of an advantage than a disadvantage, since there is almost an infinite number of outcome variables theoretically available for study in any given area. If all of these variables received equal emphasis, scientific progress as we know it would be almost impossible because we measure increases in empirical and theoretical knowledge primarily in terms of what we know about outcome variables and the interventions that influence them. If every researcher were free to choose any variable that struck his or her fancy, then our efforts would be so scattered that we might never understand the etiology of any single variable. (Actually, researchers dealing with human behavior do sometimes appear to behave in this way to a certain extent, which may be yet another reason why these disciplines have not made as much progress as they should have.)

Thus in educational research, a primary outcome variable could be the amount learned to the extent that the purpose of schooling is defined as imparting knowledge deemed necessary to function successfully in society. Any alternative outcome that a researcher wished to employ would need to bear a direct link to learning or to some other primary outcome variable. Hence research that studies eye movements of young children learning to read would qualify only if a link were first established between eye movement and, say, reading achievement. A researcher could, however, reasonably employ decreased disruptive classroom behavior, increased voluntary time on task, or decreased absences from school as outcome variables since these variables have been empirically linked to student achievement. Similarly, changes in teacher behaviors designed to affect such a variable would qualify, but attitudes toward a particular subject matter would not be a reasonable candidate unless someone had first demonstrated a link between attitudes and learning.

In health-related research, reasonable outcome variables include such things as mortality and morbidity rates, decreased pain, increased recovery time, increased quality of life, decreased costs of care (assuming finite resources), and so forth. Any other outcome variables chosen must relate in some way to direct indicators such as these; thus a study designed to increase nurses' hand-washing behaviors after seeing patients would be a reasonable variable if hand washing has been shown to decrease hospital-based infections among patients.

Every social, behavioral, and health science, in fact, has its own catalog of meaningful variables that directly or indirectly affect the quality of our lives: activities of daily living, voting records, creative behavior, compliance with therapeutic regimens, risk-taking behavior, aggressive/disruptive behavior, job performance, drug and alcohol consumption, anxiety, depression, subjective well-being, mental health, marital distress, job satisfaction, absenteeism, employee turnover, social behavior, spatial ability, critical thinking, recidivism—the list, which is shared across disciplines, is almost endless. Again, the only criterion that I suggest is that the variable you choose to study be directly related to some unequivocal individual or societal good.

Some researchers consider even this criterion unduly restrictive. They would consider the demonstration of an empirical link between an intermediary variable (e.g., nurses' hand-washing behavior) and a direct individual or societal outcome (e.g., the development of staph infections) as unnecessary as long as the prevalent theory or paradigm under which the profession operates predicts such a relationship. This is a matter of individual choice, but I suggest that it is always a good idea to test such assumptions whenever possible. The history of science is replete with examples of entire generations of careers being devoted to the assiduous study of such dead-end variables as head size. (Note that at this point we are talking about global constructs, not the specific manner in which we will measure that construct. There are, for example, literally thousands of measures of student learning and hundreds of specific ways to measure most of the other social, behavioral, and health-related outcomes mentioned above. Criteria for the selection of actual measurement instruments will be discussed later.)

The first step in selecting a meaningful outcome, then, is to make sure that you can answer one of the following questions with an unequivocal "yes." If you cannot, I suggest that you go back to the drawing board.

1. Does the outcome variable constitute a generally accepted personal or societal good (i.e., does it relate to health, happiness, or productivity)?
2. Is the outcome variable causally linked to a generally accepted personal or societal good? (For example, consumption of dietary fat would be a reasonable dependent variable to attempt to manipulate since it is related to cardiovascular disease—which in turn results in death, pain, and decreased productivity.)

If we assume a positive answer to one of these two questions, the next step in ensuring a meaningful hypothesis test naturally involves the intervention that is designed to influence this outcome:

Principle 13: **Select a theoretically justifiable independent variable that (1) is capable of being experimentally manipulated and (2) is clearly capable of influencing your outcome variable.**

Note that we are still talking in very general terms. If you are planning to do an experimental study, there is no way that you will be able to actually design your intervention at this point. Successful interventions do not spring fully developed from the researcher's head like Zeus's children. Full-blown, successful interventions never emerge from a brainstorming session. They are always suggested by theory, previous research, or extensive clinical experience. Also, they always require extensive developmental effort to work out procedural bugs and to fine-tune their various components. What I am referring to here, then, is a globally conceptualized independent variable that will later be refined into an intervention. (An *independent variable* is defined as a variable capable of "causing" changes in an outcome variable or, at the very least, one that is known to precede it in time.) Examples of independent variables in social, behavioral, and health research might be peer drug counseling, class size, patient education, biofeedback, and psychotherapy.

Regardless of the general form your global independent variable takes at this point, I suggest that you pay very close attention to the two qualifiers in Principle 13. It does little good to choose an independent variable, for example, that is not directly manipulable. An experimental study by definition requires a manipulation of some sort, and this manipulation by definition becomes the *intervention*. Thus, even though an excellent theoretical and empirical rationale exists for the relationship between smoking and lung cancer, the former would not be a reasonable choice for an intervention because it is not directly manipulable. (Given that links have been established between smoking and a plethora of important health outcomes, however, smoking cessation can and does constitute a very reasonable *outcome* variable in its own right.)

It is of equal importance that you should never select an independent variable for which there is no empirical or theoretical rationale that links it to your outcome variable. The chances that any subsequent intervention developed from it will be successful are so remote that the research community probably would not believe your results, even if you were able to demonstrate an effect.

It is important to note that everything said to this point also applies to nonexperimental research. Even if there are no plans to manipulate the independent variable, such as in the conduct of a correlational study that simply involves assessing the relationship between two variables, Principle 13 still constitutes pretty good advice. If there is no theoretical reason why your chosen variables should correlate with one another, for example, the chances are that either they will not or no one will believe your results if they do. Further, if your independent variable can never be either directly or indirectly manipulated under any imaginable conditions, then the societal relevance of any documented relationships involving it is likely to be quite restricted. (Since it is always possible that such relationships may have scientific or theoretical importance, however, I would not award Principle 13 the status of a "rule" for nonexperimental research.)

Returning to the experimental paradigm, however, and assuming that at this point you at least have an embryonic intervention in mind, I would suggest that you evaluate it by addressing the following questions:

1. Can you visualize implementing your potential intervention given the resources (e.g., types of subjects or clinical facilities) available to you? If you cannot, you should go back to the drawing board.

2. Is there some theoretical or empirical reason to believe that your potential intervention will indeed affect your outcome? Although I would absolutely require an affirmative answer to this question as a prerequisite to conducting a meaningful study, I am quite liberal regarding what a "theoretical or empirical reason" entails. Possibilities include:
   a. a formal theory that actually predicts a relationship between the variables involved,
   b. the successful use of the planned intervention involving a different outcome or a different population,
   c. the successful use of a similar intervention involving either the same or different outcomes,
   d. the results of a large-scale correlational study that demonstrated a noncausal relationship between the variable involved, or even
   e. pilot work conducted by the investigator for the very purpose of suggesting the efficacy of the intervention.

An affirmative answer to both of these questions indicates that you are now ready to formally state your research intentions, which happens to constitute the subject of the next chapter.

Suggested Readings

General References

Although general reference books have limited utility with respect to reviewing any discrete literature, there are occasions when certain factual information is required as background for a research study or when hints regarding the location of additional research studies outside the researcher's discipline may be needed. Three sources (contained in the reference sections of practically all research libraries) that may prove to be useful starting points for these purposes are:

Sheehy, E. P. (Ed.). (1986, but periodically updated). *Guide to reference books* (10th ed.). Chicago: American Library Association.
> This huge text contains general works, bibliographies, texts, and all types of reference books for just about every major academic discipline.

Towell, J. E. (Ed.). (1989). *Directories in print.* Detroit, MI: Gale.
> This is a periodically updated directory of directories that consists of an annotated guide to more than 10,000 business and industrial directories, professional and scientific rosters, directory databases, and other lists/guides.

Ulrich's International Periodical Directory (27th ed.). (Annual). New York: Bowker.
> Organized by subject, this 4,000+ page trilogy (the final volume is given over to on-line serials and an index to publications of international organizations) provides addresses, editors, telephone numbers, and circulation figures for tens of thousands of periodicals (including scholarly journals). This volume can prove useful in locating leading journals in related fields that may publish research in the topic of interest.

The Literature Review

Two useful texts specifically given over to the conduct of literature reviews are:

Cooper, H. (1984). *The integrative research review: A systematic approach.* Beverly Hills, CA: Sage.
> This brief book provides seven chapters dealing with every aspect of performing a literature review, including one titled "Methods for Locating Studies."

Light, R. J., & Pillemer, D. B. (1984). *Summing up: The science of reviewing research.* Cambridge, MA: Harvard University Press.
> Arguing that most literature reviews are too subjective to be scientifically sound, the authors provide guidelines for conducting a methodologically sound one. They also include strategies for organizing a

comprehensive reviewing strategy and provide a checklist for evaluating same.

Two of many articles that offer useful guidelines for conducting a literature review (both of which start with the explicitly stated assumption that individuals who conduct literature reviews should be just as scientifically rigorous as those who conduct experiments) are:

Cooper, H. M. (1982). Scientific guidelines for conducting integrative research reviews. *Review of Educational Research, 52,* 291-302.

Jackson, G. B. (1980). Methods for integrative reviews. *Review of Educational Research, 50,* 438-460.

Meta-Analysis

There are a number of excellent texts on meta-analytic techniques. The following is only a sampling of those available:

Glass, G. V., McGaw, R., & Smith, M. L. (1981). *Meta-analysis in social research.* Beverly Hills, CA: Sage.
> This is the classic, original text in the area and should definitely be read by anyone with a serious interest in meta-analysis. It is especially relevant to meta-analyses conducted on experimental research and, although the field has moved on considerably since the publication of this book, is still quite useful for this purpose.

Hunter, J. E., & Schmidt, F. L. (1990). *Methods of meta-analysis: Correcting error and bias in research findings.* Newbury Park, CA: Sage.
> This book should definitely be read by anyone serious in mastering the technique. At present it is undoubtedly the most complete teaching resource available on meta-analysis, although it tends to emphasize the meta-analysis of nonexperimental research.

Rosenthal, R. (1984). *Meta-analytic procedures for social research.* Beverly Hills, CA: Sage.
> This may be somewhat easier reading for beginners than Glass et al. and advocates a slightly different strategy.

For anyone interested in the potential of meta-analysis for resolving some of the problems inherent in the social, behavioral, and health sciences, the following sources might prove interesting:

Bausell, R. B. (1993). After the meta-analytic revolution. *Evaluation and the Health Professions, 16*, 3-12.

Cook, T. D., Cooper, H., Cordray, D. S., Hartmann, H., Hedges, L. V., Light, R. J., Louis, T. A., & Mosteller, F. (1992). *Meta-analysis for explanation*. New York: Russell Sage.

Schmidt, F. L. (1992). What do data really mean? Research findings, meta-analysis, and cumulative knowledge in psychology. *American Psychologist, 47*, 1173-1181.

Wachter, K. W., & Straf, M. L. (Eds.). (1990). *The future of meta-analysis*. New York: Russell Sage.

3

Formulating a Meaningful Hypothesis

It is now time to talk about the step which everything to this point has been designed to facilitate. Let us assume that the literature review has been completed (although it will always need to be updated) and the other 12 principles have been followed as well. You should now be in a position to make a formal statement of your research intentions based upon (1) an appreciation of what has been done in the area, (2) what needs to be done, and equally important, (3) what *can* be done.

This rather formidable task boils down to a series of discrete skills, which includes:

1. Being able to ascertain what can and cannot be accomplished within the context of a single empirical research study.
2. Being able to visualize the results, both with respect to the general form they will take and with respect to the different outcomes obtainable. (It is helpful, although not always essential, to be able to estimate which of these different outcomes are most likely to occur.)
3. Being able to judge the implications capable of being derived from the results, including the uses to which they can be put and the types of questions that they will in turn generate.

There are, however, three steps that precede even the application of these skills, and they are:

1. determining what one's "real" or "root" purpose for conducting the study at hand is,
2. determining what one's "scientific" purpose is for conducting the study, and
3. formulating an explicit, *operational* statement of what the question at hand is.

Although these preliminary steps are probably not necessary for experienced investigators, they deserve the status of hard-and-fast *rules* for anyone about to conduct his or her first empirical study. The first two are assumed under Principle 14:

Principle 14: **Sit down and honestly assess what your true, personal motives are for conducting the study.**

Here I am referring to your "real" motivations for conducting the particular study under consideration. I am not referring to anything that the average researcher would ever admit to in person. Instead, I am suggesting an introspective examination of motives. Examples (and it is certainly possible to have multiple agenda) might be:

1. to change a distasteful (i.e., to the researcher) professional practice,
2. to learn everything there is to know about a particular variable,
3. to discredit a theory or line of thought considered to be either wrong or archaic,
4. to test a theory to see if it is valid,
5. to lend credence to the formulation of the investigator's own theory,
6. to further one's career by conducting a seminal research study,
7. to further one's career by obtaining a "research publication,"

8. to obtain one's doctorate in order to go into a professional practice (and possibly never have to conduct research again),
9. to become famous,
10. to further scientific progress in one's discipline, or
11. simply to discover something of intellectual interest.

I am sure there are circumstances in which all of these motives are justifiable, although some may not be particularly realistic. If Motivation #9 involves getting on the cover of *People* magazine, for example, you should probably either choose another line of work or use celebrities as research subjects. Motive #2 is equally unrealistic and will probably result in a diffuse fishing expedition that produces nothing of value. Motive #8 is quite realistic but can be accomplished without bothering with the 40 rules presented here.

All the remaining motives can be realistic, but I passionately beseech you to make sure that yours are at least compatible with the conduct of meaningful research. This, it will be remembered, translates to *research that is capable of making an actual scientific contribution (which is defined as determining the causes, effects, or etiology of a phenomenon), of providing a mechanism to improve the likelihood of obtaining better clinical outcomes, or of actually helping people and furthering the human condition.*

Regardless of what one's motives are for conducting research, I think it is essential for investigators to at least be aware of what they are and to use them to evaluate explicitly how likely the studies they are planning are to satisfy them. Perhaps the most integral step in this evaluative process is the composition of a formal *operational* statement of the purpose of the study within a testable, doable format. These operational articulations of research purposes are conventionally called *hypotheses.*

Once committed to paper, a formal hypothesis is capable of forcing a researcher to confront his or her aspirations within the cold reality of what the study it represents is capable of producing, which is one of the prime rationales for Principle 15:

▼

Principle 15: **Translate your proposed study into one or more formal, written hypotheses.**

▼

Before discussing the specifics of how to do this, I should mention that there are at least three types of hypotheses. These are:

1. *null* hypotheses (which simply state that there will be no relationship or difference among the variables studied, although in fact the researcher believes, or the evidence from the literature suggests, that one does exist),
2. *research* hypotheses (which are simply the opposite side of the coin and state that there is such a relationship or difference), and
3. *directional* hypotheses (which take the research hypothesis one step further by specifying the direction of the relationship or difference).

Although each of these forms has its passionate defenders and detractors, the truth of the matter is that one is no better or worse than the other. A hypothesis should be designed solely to communicate the operational purpose of a study as succinctly as possible. As long as it is able to do this successfully, it makes no difference whether it is stated negatively or positively or what tense it is written in.

For some reason, many people seem to believe that there is one and only one "correct" way to write a hypothesis. The truth of the matter is, however, that unless Mel Brooks was correct and Moses did drop a few of his commandments on the way down from the mountain, few things in research are carved in stone. There is nothing sacred about even such widely accepted conventions that "the null hypothesis is never proved or established, but is possibly disproved, in the course of experimentation." When we trace it back to its roots, we find that this particular statement is nothing more than a philosophical preference articulated by two statisticians named Yule and Pearson. Equally credible authorities (e.g., Neyman and a different Pearson) believe that null hypotheses can be accepted if the experiments themselves are designed with sufficient sensitivity.

At the risk of my being repetitive, then, a research hypothesis is neither more nor less than a clear, concise, operational definition of a study's purpose. To be useful, such a definition must include at least some cursory information about the primary components of the study in question. It is optimal that another scientist should be able to glean pretty much what a study is all about by reading its hypothesis(es) in isolation.

This is actually a pretty tall order. If you are to accomplish this, a good hypothesis should have the following characteristics:

1. A hypothesis should consist of a statement that can be judged as either true or false. This true or false judgment, in turn, is made on the basis of a statistical analysis performed upon the data that the study itself is designed to collect. The specific analytic procedure need not be specified, but by writing a statement that can be judged as true or false (which is exactly analogous to asking a question whose answer is either "yes" or "no"), you will automatically eschew such phrases as "the best way" or "determine the meaning of" or words such as "good" or "why."

If, after formulating a hypothesis, you are unsure whether it really will be subject to a "true" or "false" decision following statistical analysis, then you may want to turn it into a research *question*. If the question can be answered either affirmatively or negatively—there are no maybes in hypothesis testing—then you have a testable hypothesis. If the question cannot be answered with a simple "yes" or "no," then your hypothesis is probably not testable unless it can be broken into multiple questions, which can be answered in this way. (Hence it is usually a good idea to write separate hypotheses when more than one outcome variable is employed and when more than one contrast between experimental interventions is planned.) If this still does not work, then you should go back to the drawing board.

2. The groups and/or variables should be specified and, where appropriate, independent versus dependent statuses should be delineated. This will be a simple task for the type of research we will be discussing in this book, because the independent variable will always be an experimental intervention that you will manipulate, and the dependent variable will be the outcome that this intervention is designed to influence.

3. When an intervention is involved, the hypothesis should be stated in terms of assessing differences (or changes) with respect to the effects of this intervention. The manner in which it was decided who would receive said intervention should also be stated, along with the type of comparison that will be used to evaluate these differences. When controlling variables (i.e., attributes that are measured before the study starts and used later to statistically "subtract out" any preexisting differences among the study's groups) or multiple administrations of the outcome variable are involved (e.g., the use of follow-up measurements), some mention should be made of these as well. In empirical research involving people, an intervention is tested either by assigning subjects to groups or by administering it to everyone in the study. When different groups are used, the identity of these groups should be described, along with a statement as to whether subjects were *randomly assigned* (i.e., where each subject was given an equal chance of receiving or not receiving the intervention in question) or there was *nonrandom assignment* (where subjects were selected in some other way). (If everyone in the study receives the intervention, then the hypothesis should state this as well.)

4. Some general mention should be made of the types of subjects employed. Since the primary purpose of a hypothesis is to communicate the essence of the study being conducted, the reader obviously needs to know whether, say, hospitalized cardiovascular patients or fifth-grade elementary school students are being employed.

There are almost as many ways to write a hypothesis as there are researchers to test it. If a hypothesis contains each of the above elements, however, then it will serve its primary purpose, which is to communicate the operational objective of the study. An example of such a hypothesis might be:

> There is a difference in fifth-grade mathematics achievement scores between students randomly assigned to receive 45 minutes of mathematics instruction per day and those assigned to receive 60 minutes of comparable instruction.

Here the sample is described (fifth-grade students), the groups/interventions delineated (i.e., students receiving longer versus shorter instructional periods), along with the manner in which it was decided who would receive which (i.e., random assignment); and the criterion (i.e., the outcome variable) by which they will be compared (a mathematics achievement test) is described. The hypothesis is also obviously capable of being accepted or rejected since it can be easily reformulated as a question that can be answered either positively or negatively:

> Is there a difference in fifth-grade mathematics achievement scores between students receiving 45 minutes of mathematics instruction per day and those receiving 60 minutes of comparable instruction?

If random assignment was not used to compare the two types of classes, the hypothesis should indicate this by omitting the "randomly assigned" portion of the hypothesis and possibly substituting something like "intact classrooms." If the students' prior mathematical abilities were to be taken into account, this fact too should be noted by tacking on "when prior mathematical ability is statistically controlled." If retrospective data were collected on a large number of classrooms, with respect to both their students' test scores and the length of their math periods, then the resulting hypothesis might read as follows:

> There is a relationship between mean fifth-grade mathematics classroom achievement scores and length of instructional periods after prior mathematics achievement has been statistically controlled.

This particular hypothesis would tell the reader that (1) a correlational study was being performed (i.e., "relationship between"); (2) the data points would be classrooms rather than individual students (i.e., "mean . . . classroom . . . scores"); (3) the length of the mathematics instructional periods was allowed to vary "naturally" (since no mention was made of any discrete time intervals); and (4) previous achievement was used as a statistical control ("after prior . . . has been statistically controlled").

Everything said here applies equally well to any social-, behavioral-, or health-related investigations, regardless of the method by which they are conducted or their subject matters. The following statement, for example, employs all of the recommended components for a good hypothesis and communicates a great deal about its parent study (even if it does become a bit wordy):

> A group counseling procedure involving empowerment techniques will result in reduced high-risk sexual behavior among methadone maintenance African-American women, as compared to a randomly assigned attention-control group, both immediately following therapy and 6 months thereafter, after prior sexual behavior has been statistically controlled.

Writing good, succinct hypotheses takes practice, but they do not have to be "perfect" or aesthetically pleasing to communicate what the study is all about as long as they (1) can be judged as true or false, (2) clearly specify the identify of all groups and/or variables employed, (3) identify the general type of design employed (e.g., whether the study in question employed an intervention to which subjects were randomly assigned, an intervention to which subjects were not randomly assigned, or was purely correlational in nature), and (4) give some indication of the types of subjects employed.

I think it is worth reiterating, however, that none of these recommendations is carved in stone. There is no "rule" that even says you have to write a hypothesis prior to conducting a study. Many experienced researchers do not. There is even no "rule" that says a hypothesis or a research question has to be written in an accept/reject—yes/no format, but this is a tried-and-tested convention that is probably worth retaining.

There is another overriding reason why it behooves a beginning researcher to adopt the above four-step strategy, however, and this is because the main beneficiary of a well-written hypothesis is the researcher himself or herself. This is because the best way to judge the potential meaningfulness of a research study is to judge the meaningfulness of the hypothesis itself prior to conducting the study in question.

Another important benefit of a clearly stated hypothesis is that it allows the researcher *to ascertain what can and cannot be accomplished within the context of a single empirical research study*. Thus, returning to the sample hypotheses above, serious contemplation of this relatively restrictive declarative sentence should point out to the researcher exactly what he/she stands to learn from the studies they represent. Assigning "true" or "false" labels to these statements will not tell us what the best way to teach mathematics or prevent AIDS is. Such labels will not tell us what the optimum length of a fifth-grade mathematics class is, nor will they tell us anything about the best type of group counseling. They will tell us nothing about other types of instruction or therapeutic modalities and they will probably not tell us much about other types of samples.

The statements' very restrictiveness will, however, enable their authors to visualize the different outcomes obtainable: That is, the 60-minute classes will result in either greater, or less, or equal mathematics achievement than the 45-minute classes; and the group therapy intervention will result in either positive, or negative, or no changes in sexual behavior when compared to the placebo group. Visualizing the restrictive nature of such outcomes can greatly facilitate the a priori evaluation of the meaningfulness of one's research hypotheses, and it is to this crucial process that the next chapter is dedicated.

Suggested Reading

For a readable description of the origins of some of the conventions regarding hypothesis testing, the types of errors one can make therein, and the controversy of whether a null hypothesis is ever accepted, I would recommend:

Binder, A. (1963). Further considerations on testing the null hypothesis and the strategy and tactics of investigating theoretical models. *Psychological Review, 70,* 105-115.

4

Evaluating the Meaningfulness of the Research Hypothesis

It is now time to attempt one of the most important, difficult, and often neglected steps in the research process: evaluating the meaningfulness of one's hypothesis(es) for the express purpose of deciding whether the parent study is worth conducting. Formulating a testable hypothesis comprised of an important outcome variable and an intervention that is theoretically capable of manipulating this outcome is a very important step. There is no guarantee, however, that the actual testing of such a hypothesis will produce results capable of:

1. generating a high quality causal inference,
2. providing a mechanism for improving the quality of someone's life, and/or
3. satisfying the researcher's personal objectives for conducting the study in the first place.

To meet all of these criteria, it is necessary to conduct a formal evaluation of the entire study as it has been formulated to this point. Hence the following principle:

▼

Principle 16: **Once the outcome variable has been chosen and the intervention developed, take the time to evaluate your research hypothesis's meaningfulness thoroughly.**

▼

As discussed in Chapter 3, there are three prerequisite skills for accomplishing this task. These, it will be remembered, were:

1. Being able to ascertain what can and cannot be accomplished within the context of a single empirical research study.
2. Being able to visualize the results, both with respect to the general form they will take and with respect to the different outcomes obtainable.
3. Being able to judge the implications that can be derived from the study's results, including the uses to which they can be put and the types of questions that they will in turn generate.

Understanding the Limitations
Inherent in the Empirical Process

The very act of writing a hypothesis will go a long way toward achieving this objective in and of itself. Delineating the exact relationship or difference to be tested, for example, can very quickly narrow one's expectations for a study's ultimate outcome since any statement that can be judged only as true or false has a rather definite built-in limitation. Similarly, the specification of the study variables has a narrowing effect and, if nothing else, specifying who will be studied underlines the limits to which the results can be generalized. I also think, however, that the acceptance of the following two tenets may prove equally useful to beginning researchers if they are directly applied to the type of detailed evaluative process being suggested here:

Tenet 1: There is only so much that can be learned from a single study, no matter how well it is designed. This is an especially difficult truism for a beginning researcher to accept, especially just after the flash of genius that has produced the hypothesis in the first place. Like it or not, however, the empirical process consists of a number of discrete, relatively small steps that ultimately must be supplemented by further studies and replicated by other researchers.

Tenet 2: It is far better to provide a definitive answer to a specific, narrow question than it is to answer a diffuse, broad question equivocally. A corollary to this is that it is better to err on the side of making the study's focus too narrow than too wide. Beginning researchers have a decided tendency to try to supply all the answers to all of the questions they can think of. The truth of the matter is, however, that whenever a researcher supplies a single definitive answer to even a small question, he or she will have been wildly successful.

Visualizing Results

Sometimes one of the hardest things for beginning researchers to accept is the fact that regardless of how great their aspirations for a study are, the ultimate outcome is going to be nothing but a few numbers accompanied by a true/false decision. An experimental study always involves a comparison of some sort of group means. The importance of the difference between these means by necessity becomes synonymous with the importance of the study itself. In the final analysis, then, something is going to be judged as greater than, less than, or the same as something else, and that is basically all that is going to accrue. The researcher's job at the hypothesis formulation stage is therefore to decide: (a) if these "somethings" are important enough to study, and (b) if it is truly important that one is greater than, less than, or the same as the other(s).

Even if the answer to both of these questions is "yes," the researcher should still decide if all of the possible outcomes of the proposed study are equally important. (It is usually the case, for example, that a nonsignificant difference resulting from the evaluation of an innovative new treatment, which no one has ever heard of, will not generate nearly as much interest as a statistically significant difference supporting its efficacy.) If one of the possible outcomes is considerably more important (or more interesting) than the others, the researcher must therefore further decide: (c) if its occurrence is sufficiently likely to justify the study.

Obviously, if the answer to either (a) or (b) is "no," then the study should not be conducted. It is often a little more difficult to evaluate the third question, but an informed guess, based upon a careful analysis of the literature, can be quite helpful here. If one of the possible outcomes is considerably less interesting than the others (e.g., if it is unlikely that a leading journal would publish a study reporting such a finding) and if it is considerably more likely to occur than the others, then conducting the study is a risk that may not be worth taking unless the stakes are quite high (i.e., the less likely results would be very important if they should accrue).

When the literature is not helpful in assessing the probability of a particular outcome (e.g., when new treatments and/or variables are being studied), the most likely outcome by far for any given study is *no significant difference between groups*. Unfortunately it is almost always the case that this happens to also be the least interesting possible outcome as far as the rest of the scientific community is concerned. (Chapter 6 is specifically devoted to ways of decreasing the likelihood of your obtaining nonsignificant differences between your groups.)

Judging Implications of Results

Judging the implications of one's results is synonymous with answering the infamous "So what?" question. It is perhaps the most difficult and subjective step in the entire evaluative process, but it is such an important skill that its mastery should be pursued tenaciously. Some strategies for facilitating this task follow:

1. Try to assess honestly (Principle 14) what your true personal objectives are for the study. Again, I am not referring here to the words that appear in the research hypothesis; rather, I am suggesting an honest attempt to come to grips with one's internal motivations. I consider this step important because it may reveal an objective that simply cannot be accomplished. Even if one's true goal is nothing more ambitious than just to publish a research study, an understanding of this can itself be helpful since some types of hypotheses lend themselves more readily to publication than others.

2. Rethink each element of the hypothesis in view of the answer to 1. In other words, are the choices made regarding outcomes, interventions, and/or the target sample appropriate? (For example, will other researchers be interested in the experimental intervention you have chosen or in the measuring instruments you have selected to compare them upon? Are the types of subjects you have chosen to employ the most interesting available?)

3. Try to visualize how each of the possible study outcomes fits into the previous research literature. Said another way, how likely is it that the results of this study would be published by the types of journals that appear in your reference list? Unpublished research is of little benefit to anyone.

4. In relation to 3, what would the next study be based upon each of these possible outcomes? Later I will suggest that you write follow-up hypotheses to fit these results. Studies that do not generate meaningful questions for future research may not be worth conducting.

5. Actually ask the "So what?" question and attempt to answer it honestly with respect to previous research, relevant theories, and potential applications. If the study is designed to test a theory, then this test should be conducted in terms of identifying the etiology of a specific phenomenon. A good theory should predict that a particular phenomenon will occur under certain specific conditions, so the study in question should be designed to ascertain whether this prediction is correct or incorrect. (Be prepared for the fact, however, that most people will still believe the theory, regardless of your results.) If the theory is not specific enough to derive such hypotheses, as most are not in the social, behavioral, and health sciences, then it is probably not worth testing. Similarly, if the study is designed to change a professional practice, its results should be capable of providing evidence that the practice in question is either harmful or inferior to a proposed alternative or, at the very least, the equivalent of a much cheaper/less invasive procedure. (Again, be prepared for the fact that the practice in question will probably linger on until other scientists replicate your study or until some non-empirical impediment is raised to it.) If the study is designed to improve the human condition somehow (e.g., by helping people live longer, be happier, be healthier, or be more productive), then its results should be capable of providing guidance toward the accomplishment of same. As always, this guidance may very well be ignored, but your job as a scientist is to point the way toward a better world, even if you can't single-handedly change the present one. (*If the study has no implications at all for improving the human condition, then you might want to consider whether it is worth conducting at all.*)

6. Pose as many alternative hypotheses for the study's potential outcomes as possible. These alternative hypotheses should be both methodologically (more will be said about these later) and logically generated. Always ascribe to "Occam's razor," which suggests that complex explanations should never be substituted for simpler ones unless the latter can be categorically shown to be inferior. Also, be aware of the major paradigm (see Thomas Kuhn's *The Structure of Scientific Revolutions*, University of Chicago Press, 1962) in which you are operating and make sure that it is consonant with your hypothesis. It is also often a good idea to at least consider the possibility that this same paradigm may be blinding you from choosing a potentially even more effective intervention.

7. Prepare a formal defense of 5 and 6, assuming a hostile audience. A good way to do this is to assume that you are going to have to present your study at a press conference composed of skeptical journalists who are largely ignorant of your discipline. This will prepare you for the next step, which involves facing the most hostile audience of all.

Soliciting the Help of Colleagues

Only after all of the above steps have been conscientiously followed do I recommend that you get outside help in evaluating your hypothesis. (An exception might be if you have a close friend who is conversant with the area in question.) It can be very helpful to have a sounding board upon which to try out your research ideas, but I suggest that you do your homework first and attempt to line up professionals who have conducted research in the area of interest or who are thoroughly familiar with the research literature(s) and the issues involved.

If possible, actually arrange to present your proposed study to a group of colleagues willing to take the time to critique its importance. This provides an excellent opportunity to obtain independent opinions as well as valuable procedural/methodological suggestions. Many academic settings provide a mechanism for such forums in the form of brown-bag colloquia or journal clubs. (Doctoral students have a built-in mechanism of this sort in the form of their dissertation committee, although I personally suggest a dry run with independent parties prior to this particular experience.)

Regardless of who you line up to hear your proposal, suggest that your audience be critical from the onset. You should probably come prepared to argue for the meaningfulness of your hypotheses (and you should come prepared to be thick-skinned), but most of all view for this process as an opportunity to improve your study (in other words, prepare to be flexible).

If, after this experience, you remain convinced of your study's worth, then you should probably go ahead and conduct it, even if your colleagues turn out to be less than enthusiastic. If you are unconvinced following all of this, however, I would suggest that you go back to the drawing board.

Limitations of Professional Feedback

The above suggestions for soliciting outside help in evaluating the meaningfulness of one's research hypotheses really only apply to beginning researchers who are in the process of learning how to answer the "So what?" question for themselves. There are many drawbacks to this practice, not the least of which is the difficulty of getting honest, unemotional feedback from people who have their own agenda to fulfill. The most common failing in this regard is of people not wanting to appear overly critical and therefore being less than honest in their assessments. Negative opinions too can be wrong (one relatively common academic trait, in fact, involves always being aggressively negative), so the best you can hope for in soliciting this type of help is that someone will bring up a point (or will suggest a procedural improvement) that you have not previously thought of.

Personally, I think I will always remember my late-night completion of the data analysis for a study I had just concluded, in which elementary class size was experimentally manipulated under controlled conditions for the first time. In addition to achieving statistical significance in all the predicted ways, the results formed an almost perfect logarithmic curve, which compelled me to try to find someone with whom to share this exciting piece of information. This someone happened to be the first person I ran into in the corridor, who also happened to be a methodologically sophisticated individual with little appreciation for schooling research. His response to my breathless description of what I considered to be a major breakthrough was a bored "So what? Schools don't have enough money to reduce their class sizes so nobody is going to be able to use your results."

I was shocked. To that point there had been literally hundreds of class size studies, but no one had ever bothered to study the phenomenon in a laboratory situation, where variables such as teacher and student differences, instructional time, and exactly what was taught during this time could be rigorously controlled. As a result, the overall judgment from this literature was equivocal, with the best guess among the research community being that class size either did not result in improved learning or, if it did, that the effect was trivial in size. (Public school teachers, of course, always knew that class size was an extremely important determinant of how much children learned in school.)

What I had set out to do, then, was demonstrate that smaller class sizes *could* result in increased learning, when all relevant extraneous variables were controlled, and this I had accomplished admirably. Without my belaboring the point, this particular study would certainly appear to have met most of the above criteria for meaningfulness, so why did my colleague come up with such a diametrically opposing judgment?

I've always found ascribing motivations to people a most tenuous enterprise, but there are several possibilities—all of which are relevant to the issue of soliciting outside, a priori judgments regarding the meaningfulness of a research hypothesis. In the first place, of course, he was judging the study on one and only one criterion, so it is important to at least recognize the different perspectives by which your study can be judged. It is even more important that you should explicitly recognize the criteria you have used to judge the meaningfulness of your own study. (You should always be aware of the possibility that you have made an inappropriate selection in this regard.)

Another possibility that must also always be considered, when professionals render opinions regarding work other than their own, is the presence of professional jealousy, insecurity, or simple pique at the presumptuousness (or threat) of someone else claiming to have just conducted (or is planning to conduct) a seminal study. These factors are things that all researchers must contend with at some point, since, if nothing else, their completed work will be subjected to professional judgment when it is submitted for publication. The fact that unbiased, honest judgments are sometimes difficult to obtain, however, does not mean that such judgments are not worth pursuing. On the contrary, they are so valuable that it behooves you to make the extra effort needed to obtain them. This can often be done via the following simple steps:

   a. assume (or at least affect, if it doesn't come naturally) a healthy dose of humility when dealing with one's colleagues,

b. assure them that you truly do want a frank assessment of your work,
c. accept criticism graciously and gratefully (even if you consider it moronic), and
d. take the time to supply unbiased, honest (but diplomatic) feedback yourself when requested.

Subjectivity and Meaningfulness

Perhaps the greatest inherent limitation in all of the strategies in this chapter resides in the ultimate subjectivity of the concept of meaningfulness. In the final analysis, what is meaningful to one person may be completely trivial to another.

The ultimate arbiter of meaningfulness is what stands the test of time and what does not. Some studies contribute to science; the vast majority do not. All I am trying to do here is enhance the probability that your study will make such a contribution. Barring this, my second objective is to enhance the probability that you will conduct a study that you are personally proud of, which in the long run may be of equal importance.

To return to my personal experiences, over the years I have not changed my opinion about the meaningfulness of my class size study (or of a number of other unmentioned schooling studies I conducted around the same time). I think of this work as an artist must think of one of his or her favorite paintings. I will always remember its conduct and the experience of analyzing the resulting data and learning something that, for one brief shining moment, no one else in the world had ever known. This was a decidedly aesthetic experience that I have known only two other times during the course of a career that has spanned many more than 100 studies.

I mention this because I think it is important to realize early in one's career that there are definite limits to the external rewards that a researcher can reap from a single study (or even a program of research). Thus, while my class size study was cited a number of times, that was about all the external reinforcement I received from it. It did not even come close to closing the book on this line of research. It took Gene Glass and Mary Smith's seminal meta-analysis of the class size literature to do that, at least to the extent that things are ever laid to rest in science. There remains a surprising number of educational specialists out there who still think class size does not influence student learning, which is not atypical, as illustrated by the following quote, attributed to James

Clark Maxwell: "There are two theories of the nature of light, the corpuscle theory and the wave theory; we used to believe in the corpuscle theory; now we believe in the wave theory because all who believed in the corpuscle theory have died."

As a beginning researcher, you should at least be aware of the fact that your study (even if it is important and well designed) may lie hidden in the journal in which you publish it. Someone someday may come along and "discover" it, popularize it, or extend it, but even here the rewards are transitory. I have had research presented at news conferences and even summarized in those ubiquitous graphs in *USA Today*, but all of this tends to die down in a day or two and then it is over.

What is not transitory, however, is the aesthetic experience that accrues from completing and publishing a high-quality, meaningful piece of work that at least has the potential of leading to a set of important conclusions that cannot be ignored. What is also not transitory is the excitement of the search for the answer to an important question or the race to find the missing piece to a particularly intriguing puzzle. The fact that a successful conclusion to such a quest will only point the way to the next piece of the puzzle only increases the excitement of the overall enterprise. In the final analysis I think Jonas Salk summed up the scientific reward system better than anyone else ever did when he said that "The reward for good work is the opportunity to do more."

Suggested Readings

Undoubtedly the most influential article ever written on this topic remains:

Platt, J. R. (1964). Strong inference. *Science, 146*, 347-353.

> In addition to exploring the question of why some fields progress so much more rapidly than others, this article takes on the task of judging the meaningfulness of research hypotheses. Using fields such as molecular biology and high-energy physics as case studies, the author argues that it is the systematic application of inductive (or strong) inference dating back to Francis Bacon that distinguishes these fields. In his words: "Strong inference consists of applying the following steps to every problem in science, formally and explicitly and regularly: (1) Devising alternative hypotheses; (2) Devising a crucial experiment (or several of them), with alternative possible outcomes, each of which will, as nearly as possible, exclude one or more of the hypotheses; (3) Carrying out the experi-

ment so as to get a clean result; (4) Recycling the procedure making subhypotheses or sequential hypotheses to refine the possibilities that remain." In this vein, the author suggests that the essence of scientific thought resides in two questions asked of anyone (including oneself) who either puts forth a theory ("But sir, what experiment could *dis*prove your hypothesis?") or describes an experimental study ("But sir, what hypothesis does your experiment *dis*prove?").

The next citation, mentioned in the text, should be required reading for all scientists. It is most famous for its emphasis upon the importance of paradigms, but its importance is far more reaching than that:

Kuhn, T. S. (1962). *The structure of scientific revolutions.* Chicago: University of Chicago Press.

5

Designing an Experiment

Let us assume that you have conscientiously followed all of the advice tendered to this point. Among other things this means that you have:

1. selected a meaningful outcome variable,
2. developed a theoretically promising intervention,
3. formulated a hypothesis to reflect the relationship between the two, and
4. evaluated this hypothesis's meaningfulness.

The next step involves setting up your proposed study so that a definitive "true" or "false" judgment can be obtained for the hypothesis you have so thoughtfully constructed.

This process is called *designing the study* and it entails considering such questions as:

1. Should a control or comparison group be employed?
2. If so, how many should be employed and how should subjects be assigned to them?
3. What types of subjects should be used?
4. How many subjects should be employed?
5. How should these subjects be measured?

6. How many times should they be measured?
7. How long should the intervention last?
8. How should the integrity of the design be ensured?
9. What steps should be taken to ensure that the relationship between the intervention and outcome variable is "real" and not an artifact of the study's design itself?

If the correct decisions are made when answering these questions, then the researcher has an excellent chance of arriving at a true determination of whether his or her hypothesis is correct. Unfortunately, one single inappropriate decision made at any of these steps is capable of rendering an entire study worthless, regardless of the meaningfulness of the hypothesis being tested. For this simple but obvious reason, it behooves you to design your study with exceeding care. This chapter is designed to facilitate this process and will begin with the most important advice of all:

▼

Principle 17: **When conducting an experiment, always employ a control (or comparison) group and always randomly assign subjects to both it and the intervention group.**

▼

There are 40 principles in this book and they all pale in significance to this one. The purpose of just about all socially meaningful scientific research is to demonstrate causal relationships between independent (in our case interventions) and dependent (outcome) variables. If we are members of one of the health professions, we need to know how to cure or prevent diseases, improve our patients' functional status, hasten their recovery, lessen their pain, or improve the quality of their lives. If we are educators, we need to know how to help children learn more and even what to teach them in order to increase their chances of enjoying self-fulfilling lives. If we are political scientists, we need to know how people make decisions and what influences these decision-making processes. If we are psychologists or sociologists, we need to know why people behave the way they do, how to increase certain types of behavior, and how to prevent others.

All of these objectives require the generation of causal evidence of one form or another. We need, in other words, to know that our interventions cause changes in our outcomes. Conservative investigators will sometimes not admit that this is the real purpose of their research, but the truth of the matter is that causal evidence is almost always a necessary condition of meaningfulness itself.

The surest way to produce evidence that an intervention (i.e., the curative, preventive, or facilitative strategy of interest) is causally related to an *outcome* variable (i.e., the socially/personally/professionally relevant dimension that needs to be changed) is to compare the effect on the outcome variable of interest between those individuals who receive an intervention to those who do not. If a relatively small number of other precautions are then taken, the researcher will have demonstrated that any observed relationship is indeed causal.

By giving everyone who agrees to participate in a study an equal chance of either receiving an intervention or not receiving it, random assignment helps to ensure the initial equivalency of all the groups employed. This is extremely important, since it protects against the possibility that one of the groups contained subjects that either (a) were superior on the outcome variable to begin with or (b) possessed a greater propensity to change over time. Either possibility is perfectly capable of invalidating an entire study, either by producing *false positive* results (e.g., when the intervention is really ineffective, but superior subjects were assigned to it at the onset of the study) or *false negative* results (e.g., the intervention was really effective, but the control groups received the bulk of the superior subjects).

Research that does not protect against the possibility that subjects who receive an intervention are systematically different from those who do not produces such weak causal evidence, in fact, that the majority of the scientific community categorically refuses to allow anything approaching the meaning of causation to slip into descriptions of the results. (This is true regardless of whether a correlational design is employed or the researcher introduces an intervention but does not randomly assign subjects thereto.) It is therefore due to two related facts that I place so much emphasis upon Principle 17:

1. Very few individuals would bother to conduct research if they did not really believe that they were bringing some causal evidence to bear on the topics that interest them.

2. The most consistently scientifically acceptable way of producing causal evidence is to randomly assign subjects to receive either a treatment or some alternative to it and then to measure the resultant effect on this manipulation.

Monitoring the Random Assignment Process

Given the preeminent importance of the random assignment process in the design of experiments, I offer the following advice for anyone seriously contemplating conducting one:

1. Never delegate the actual assignment process to anyone else (unless perhaps he or she is a research methodologist). I offer this advice because few nonresearchers are able to appreciate the importance of randomly assigning subjects to groups. I have no idea why this is so, except perhaps that there is something demeaning to some people about repeatedly flipping a coin, tossing a die, or writing down entries from a table of random numbers. Whatever the reason, I counsel against allowing someone who does not have a personal stake in the investigation to carry out this particular task. It is simply too important to trust to anyone else and it is definitely too important to delegate to, say, a busy clinician who has other responsibilities.

2. Regardless of who carries out the process, check it to make sure that it worked. Since random assignment does not guarantee the initial equivalence of intervention versus comparison groups, it is always a good idea to monitor the process whenever possible. In the next chapter I will suggest always employing additional variables (Principle 27) to increase the likelihood of supporting one's primary hypothesis. These same variables can also be used to either facilitate or check on the efficacy of the random assignment process. Thus, if gender is hypothesized to be related to the study's outcome variable, the researcher can use it as a *blocking* variable by simply randomly assigning males and females separately to intervention versus control groups. (This will ensure that males and females are represented in exact proportions across treatment groups.) If a *covariate* (i.e., a variable that will later be used for statistical control purposes, but which is not used in the random assignment process) is employed, the researcher can randomly assign subjects to intervention and comparison groups and then compare them with respect to their mean covariate values. If they differ significantly, the random assignment process can be repeated. Should all of the subjects not be available at the start of the study (e.g., they must be randomly assigned as they are admitted to a particular clinical setting), then the ratio of subjects assigned to different values of either the covariates or the blocking variables can be altered throughout the experiment via one of the many adaptive allocation methods available for this purpose.

Correlational Studies

The vast majority of studies conducted in the social and behavioral fields do not manipulate their independent variables. I generally consider this a mistake, but as discussed in Chapter 1, there is no question that there are circumstances under which very meaningful research can be conducted employing correlational designs. Some of these have been alluded to earlier but deserve repeating:

1. Nonmanipulable independent variables. Some of society's most important variables are basically nonmanipulable in nature, and I certainly do not suggest that such concerns not be the subject of empirical scrutiny.

Prime examples might be the effects of tobacco and asbestos inhalation. Even if it were not patently unethical to randomly assign individuals to inhale or not inhale such substances, the resultant effects take so long to manifest themselves that experiments involving human subjects are intrinsically impractical. No one (outside of the respective industries that produce these products), however, would argue that the research programs, which have by now generated a completely plausible causal link between such inhalation and lung cancer, are not meaningful. Any program of research that has the potential of saving lives is by definition meaningful.

I would still maintain that studies such as this are not good choices for beginning researchers, however, since they typically require large sample sizes and sophisticated statistical control techniques. (At the very least the beginning researcher should be aware of the intricacies involved in this genre of research before undertaking it.)

2. Research designed to suggest a causal link between dependent/outcome variables. As discussed above, the first and most important criterion for ensuring meaningfulness is the use of an appropriate outcome variable.

Often, however, the most important individual and societal variables are also the most difficult to study directly—sometimes because they take so long to manifest themselves; sometimes because they are relatively insensitive to direct manipulation; and sometimes because they are very difficult or expensive to measure.

As an example, the true purposes of schooling children are probably things such as increasing their productivity later on in life; making their lives more meaningful; and teaching them to shape their government to meet their individual, social, and possibly even evolutionary needs. It is very difficult to conduct research that uses children as subjects, however, but then waits until they are adults to collect such measures. What we must do in cases such as this is either accept an outcome variable based upon short-term objectives or demonstrate a correlational link between it and those long-term indicators in which we are truly interested. Such studies (which typically employ correlational designs) can be helpful if they are capable of identifying valid short-term outcome variables whose manipulation ultimately results in improvements in the human condition.

3. Research designed to suggest efficacious interventions. Another type of important preliminary work is research designed to identify or refine potential interventions for experimental research. Sometimes intervention studies are so expensive to undertake (in terms of either money or subjects' time) that funding agencies, dissertation committees, or even institutional review boards may not be willing to support a study in which some preliminary empirical data is not presented supporting the intervention's efficacy. In such cases it may be quite helpful to demonstrate a correlational link between one's chosen outcome and some approximation of the naturally occurring variable that the researcher wishes to manipulate.

Consider, for example, a study designed to test the effectiveness of self-efficacy training in allowing chronically overweight individuals to lose weight (and subsequently maintain that weight loss). Although the researcher proposing this study could cite Bandura's self-efficacy theory as a rationale for his or her intervention, a funding agency might be reluctant to finance such an experiment with no empirical link between the self-efficacy construct and weight loss. If our hypothetical researcher could demonstrate a relationship between perceived self-efficacy to lose weight and either current body weight or past weight loss success, however, then this evidence could serve as a powerful rationale for the planned experimental study, especially if as many extraneous variables as possible were statistically controlled.

There is no question, therefore, that extremely meaningful nonexperimental research can be performed. There is also no question that such research, when properly performed, can lead to reasonably high-quality causal inferences. I remain an advocate of experimental research whenever it is feasible, however, since performing a correlational study often only postpones the inevitable. Even independent variables such as cigarette smoking eventually get subjected to experimental manipulation using animal models, and the resulting evidence is often seen as more conclusive (at least by some researchers) than even the largest and most carefully designed correlational studies.

I will not belabor this point further, however. I would suggest that the researcher who intends to conduct a credible correlational study plan to:

1. employ large numbers of subjects,
2. spend as much time as necessary in identifying as many potentially confounding variables as possible to use for statistical control purposes, and
3. read the text that follows anyway, since, although it is geared exclusively to experimental studies, it is still relevant to the types of statistical controls that will be needed to give such a design at least a chance of producing credible results.

Quasi-Experimental Studies

Some studies involve the introduction of an intervention but either do not employ control groups per se or do not randomly assign subjects to them, even if one is present. Such studies are still experiments in the sense that they involve a procedural manipulation of some sort, but the quality of the causal inferences they are able to produce is severely limited by the absence of random assignment (Principle 17).

There are, in fact, five basic models for conducting an experimental study, although each contains a multitude of variants and combinations. These are:

Generic Model #1—The single-group intervention model, in which, as illustrated in Figure 5.1, all subjects are:

a. pretested on the outcome variable(s),
b. administered the intervention, and
c. posttested on the outcome variable(s).

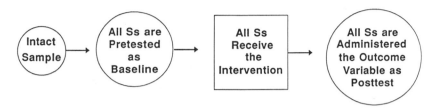

Figure 5.1. The Single-Group Intervention Model

This design is so problematic that it was not even graced with the "quasi" prefix by Donald Campbell and Julian Stanley, the originators of the terms most often used to describe experimental designs. They aptly called it a "pre-experimental" design, and since it possesses no means for controlling any of the most virulent and commonly occurring experimental artifacts that conspire to invalidate our experiments, I would categorically advise against its use. It may, in fact, be better not to conduct research at all than to employ such a weak strategy because, as will be discussed later, subjects have a natural tendency to systematically change as a function of time.

Generic Model #2—The single-group time series model, in which (see Figure 5.2) all subjects are:
a. measured repeatedly prior to the implementation of the intervention,
b. administered the same intervention(s), and
c. measured repeatedly thereafter.

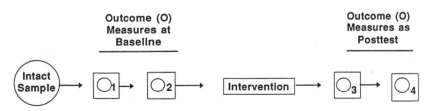

Figure 5.2. The Single-Group Time Series Model

Figure 5.3. Single-Group Time Series Model With Multiple Interventions

This design, while far from optimal, can produce reasonably high-quality causal inferences under certain conditions. Its logic revolves around the supposition that a statistically significant change will be observed following the intervention, after which the effect will begin to dissipate. If this occurs, and if no similar effect occurs at any of the other multiple measurement points, then it can be inferred that the intervention caused this change, as long as no other explanation can be advanced.

The weakness of the design, of course, resides in the fact that something other than the intervention could have caused this observed change. If the intervention is administered more than once, however, and if the same effect accrues each time it is introduced (see Figure 5.3), then considerably more confidence in the original inference is generated. (Such designs can, of course, be used only for interventions that are transitory and outcome variables that return to baseline values relatively quickly.)

Generic Model #3—The two (or more)-group model employing nonrandom assignment (see Figure 5.4), in which:

a. all subjects are either pretested or measured on one or more covariates,

b. one intact group of subjects (e.g., patients in Hospital X) is selected to receive the intervention while another group (patients in Hospital Y) is selected to serve as the control (subjects should never be allowed to select themselves into the intervention or control conditions), and

c. all subjects are administered the outcome measure as a posttest.

This design, along with its many variants, is the most commonly employed quasi-experimental design. Its main disadvantage lies in the fact that no one can ever be sure that the subjects that wind up in the nonrandomly assigned conditions (be they matched on some variable or simply happen to already be assigned to intact, preexisting groups) are equivalent to begin with.

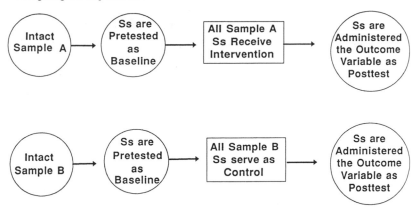

Figure 5.4. Two-Group Model Employing Nonrandom Assignment of Subjects (or Intact Groups)

The more care exercised in ensuring that these groups are initially equivalent, the more confidence can be had in one's results. I would therefore suggest that anyone employing this genre of quasi-experimental design take the following steps:

1. Employ as many subjects as possible. Not only will this help to ensure statistical power (Principle 23), but it will facilitate the statistical control that is so essential to quasi-experimental designs. It will also allow the grouped data to be broken down into different strata (e.g., males versus females, more highly educated versus less highly educated subjects) to help ensure that any achieved results are not a function of having more of one type of subject in one group than the other.

2. Actively search for possible areas of nonequivalence prior to beginning the study. If different institutions, clinics, classrooms, hospital floors, or other types of intact groups are employed for the experimental groups, assume the presence of some sort of nonequivalence and attempt to document same. Do not simply compare the groups on sociodemographic variables such as age, sex, and education. Also attempt to locate differences in the way in which the subjects are treated as a function of membership in these intact groups. Interview subjects and the staff that deals with them and view institutional records when relevant. If something surfaces that potentially gives one group a better chance to change on the outcome variable than the other, find another source of subjects that does not contain these built-in differences. Document all sources of differences and similarities prior to the beginning of the study.

3. When possible employ multiple intact groups for each experimental treatment. This, when coupled with Suggestion 2, will help to vitiate the possibility of initial nonequivalence among study subjects.

4. When Suggestion 3 is not possible, employ more than one intact group as a control. Should the group receiving the intervention exhibit greater change on the outcome than all of these groups, then more confidence can be had in the study's results.

5. Collect as much information as possible so that you will have potential controlling variables for the data analysis stage. (These can be anything that is related to the outcome variable or to the propensity to change on the outcome variable.) Baseline measures on the outcome variable should always be collected prior to implementing the treatment for this design, but so too should anything else conceivably associated with this outcome.

6. Follow Principles 18 to 37 as conscientiously as possible. Good quasi-experimental research is considerably more difficult to conduct than is research employing random assignment. It is still possible to generate reasonably high-quality inferences from such designs, however, if these principles are conscientiously implemented.

Generic Model #4—The two (or more)-group counterbalanced model in which all groups receive all of the experimental conditions (see Figure 5.5), where:

  a. two or more groups of subjects are designated (preferably randomly) to receive the experimental treatments in different orders,
  b. baseline (pretest) measures are obtained on all subjects in all groups,
  c. each experimental treatment is administered to its designated group,
  d. all subjects are measured again immediately following the experimental treatments,
  e. after sufficient time has elapsed for the outcome measure to return to its original baseline value, all subjects are measured a third time,

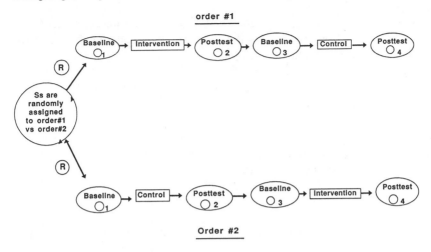

Figure 5.5. Two-Group Crossover Design

    f. the experimental treatments are again administered, although each group receives a different one than before, and

    g. all subjects are measured immediately following this implementation of the experimental treatments.

This is the strongest of the quasi-experimental designs when two very tenuous conditions can be met:

    a. there is no learning curve or practice effect for the outcome variable (in other words, administering this measure once will not affect subsequent measurements, as is the case for parameters such as blood pressure and body weight but is not the case for most affective and cognitive measures), and

    b. the potential effects of the intervention(s) are quite transitory and possess no carryover effects (which is the case for certain types of medication but is not the case for most social and behavior interventions).

Given the nature of these two assumptions, this particular design is not a good choice for most experiments conducted in the social and behavioral arenas. When they can be met, however, crossover designs can prove a powerful and efficient way of conducting research when the random assignment of subjects to treatments is not possible. (Optimal crossover designs still employ the random assignment of subjects to see who gets which treatment first.)

Generic Model #5—The two (or more)-group model employing random assignment, in which:

  a. all subjects are either pretested or measured on a covariate,
  b. subjects are randomly assigned to receive either the intervention(s) or the control(s) conditions, and
  c. all subjects are measured on the outcome variable.

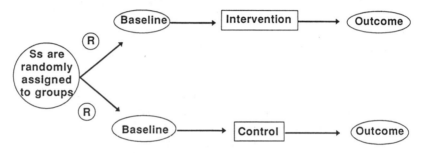

Figure 5.6. Two-Group Model Employing Random Assignment

Campbell and Stanley called studies that employed this model (and its many variations, all of which involved the random assignment of subjects to different experimental groups) "true" experiments. True experimental designs such as this are the gold standard of experimental research and should be employed by anyone seriously interested in performing serious experimental science, unless practical considerations absolutely prohibit their use.

Recommendations

There are many, many variants for each of these models. A time series design, for example, often employs two groups, in which case it becomes a combination of Model #3, #4, or #5 (see Figures 5.4, 5.5, and 5.6). Similarly, the simple randomly assigned model depicted above can

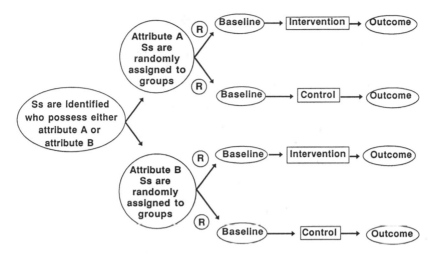

Figure 5.7. Factorial Model Employing Random Assignment

employ multiple groups that receive each treatment, in which case it becomes a factorial design, such as depicted in Figure 5.7.

Generally speaking, however, these five generic data collection models constitute the choices that social, behavioral, and health scientists have to work with in the design of their experiments. Even though every experiment has unique elements, it is possible to make some general recommendations regarding the preferability of these various designs:

1. When feasible (and, as will be discussed below, it usually is) always opt for designs that employ the random assignment of subjects to intervention and control groups. When their assumptions can be clearly met (and these should be tested via pilot studies), crossover designs in which subjects are randomly assigned to treatment order are reasonable alternatives.

2. When random assignment of subjects is not possible, utilize a quasi-experimental design (Model #4) in which intact groups are employed as the intervention and control treatments. Adopt this strategy as a last resort, however, and pay especially close attention to the guidelines listed above. Also adhere to the principles that follow in this and the next chapter very closely. They all apply to this genre of experimental design and, if anything, are even more crucial in the absence of random assignment. Above all, be extremely cautious, for quasi-experimental research

is one of the most difficult types of research to do well. (Also, be aware of the fact that about the best that researchers employing such designs can hope for is that their results will be taken seriously enough to induce someone to conduct a true experiment later on that does employ the random assignment of subjects, which leads to the question: Why not conduct *the* definitive study to begin with?)

3. There are occasions when time series models (of which there are probably more variations than any other type of design) are reasonable alternatives, but these are quite rare. They are most helpful for single-subject studies and for retrospective studies (neither of which is considered in this book). I would therefore recommend that these designs not be employed by beginning researchers without direct access to an experienced collaborator, and even here I would suggest that in most cases stronger options exist.

4. There are really very few, if any, occasions when pre-experimental designs (e.g., Model #1) are reasonable alternatives. I therefore do not recommend their use for experimental research and suggest that any researcher who cannot opt for a quasi- or true experimental alternative consider conducting nonexperimental (e.g., correlational) research instead.

On the Feasibility of Random Assignment

One of the main reasons given for not employing random assignment of subjects to groups is its unfeasibility in practice settings (or in the "real world"). I would suggest that 9 times out of 10 this is a cop-out. It is true that a certain amount of intuitive resistance to random assignment exists among the nonresearch community, especially among people who have chosen one of the helping professions as their life work. There is something cold and uncaring about choosing who will and will not receive a potentially helpful treatment on no other basis than a coin flip or a roll of the die. It is also often quite uncomfortable for a clinician to contemplate this randomization procedure, both from the impersonal perspectives of allowing chance to determine clients' access to a potentially beneficial treatment and to the admission that he or she doesn't really have all the answers regarding the optimal treatments available.

There is also something inherently unappealing about the concept for administrators. What if some clients or their families complain about the group assignment, for example? What if the process is disruptive to normal operating procedures? Why go to all of this trouble when "anyone can see" that Clinic X is the same as Clinic Y, hence that the clients in one can serve as the intervention group and the clients in the other as the control?

Suffice it to say that the manifold beauties of random assignment are not obvious to nonresearchers. This means that it is the researcher's job to convey the preeminent importance of this procedure. Some tacks that I have found helpful in these regards are:

1. Logic. Explain that the purpose of the study is to find out if the intervention does indeed work. If it does not, comparison subjects miss nothing by not being exposed to it. If a comparison group is not used, moreover, the effectiveness (or lack thereof) of the intervention may never be determined.

2. Giving everyone a chance to receive the intervention by delaying its implementation. Depending upon the setting, both treatment professionals and their administrators seem to have considerable trouble with the concept of giving half of their clients the benefit of a potentially beneficial (or simply interesting) treatment while denying the other half the same opportunity. When this concern is pervasive, the researcher can always propose a design in which subjects will be randomly assigned to receive either the intervention or the control for the necessary time interval, after which the control subjects will be offered the opportunity to benefit from the treatment.

The disadvantage of this procedure resides in the fact that it takes the researcher twice as long and requires twice the work. It does remove most of the inherent objections to random assignment, however, and it also provides a second, nonexperimental replication of the original effect (i.e., the control group's progress from the end of the first experiment to the end of their delayed intervention can be visualized as a one-group pretest-posttest design and analyzed accordingly).

3. Design the study procedures so that the random assignment of subjects is minimally disruptive. Administrators and staff can be quite helpful here, once they truly understand the concepts involved; but the researcher should at least do the groundwork by suggesting procedures that will require a minimum of adjustment by both staff and potential subjects. Often some disruption is necessary, such as physically reassigning subjects to different locations during the course of the study or reassigning intact groups, but such changes are usually possible and are often perceived by subjects as a welcome change of routine.

4. Purposefully choosing too large a setting or subject pool. If a researcher (or administrator) cannot physically (or fiscally) administer an intervention to everyone eligible to receive it, then pressure is considerably reduced to try to service everyone. What more equitable and democratic way of choosing who will and will not receive the intervention than by giving everyone an equal (or random) chance?

5. Making the control group more attractive. One of the most pervasive objections to a randomly assigned control group involves those situations in which subjects receive no treatment at all. When the comparison group can receive "treatment as usual," such as normal classroom instruction in a school or the standard medical protocol in a hospital, then many ethical and political objections tend to dissipate. (Although a bit Machiavellian, reminding an administrator of how good his or her program already is doesn't hurt here, either.) When this is not possible (or not enough), jazzing up the control group to receive interesting but irrelevant activities (or a treatment that has some face validity, but is known not to influence the outcome variable) can accomplish the same objective.

What Random Assignment Does and Does Not Do

As important as the random assignment of subjects to groups is in protecting the ultimate inferential validity of a study, it really accomplishes only one relatively simple function. *Random assignment helps to ensure that the subjects within each group are comparable to each other prior to the introduction of the intervention.* This is an extremely important function, however, because it avoids an entire class of extraneous factors that are capable of masquerading as an intervention effect.

Unfortunately, the random assignment of subjects to groups does not guard against all types of experimental artifacts. In an educational study, for example, it would do no good at all to randomly assign subjects to groups if experimental conduction were taught by an excellent teacher and control condition were taught by a poor one. For this reason the random assignment process must be supplemented by two other steps. The first of these constitutes our 18th principle:

▼

Principle 18: **In addition to randomly assigning subjects to groups, always avoid confounding any other variables with the experimental treatments.**

▼

The underlying logic of the design component of any experimental study is to set up the intervention(s) versus control(s) comparison(s) in such a way that the two groups differ only with respect to the intervention(s) involved. Every design decision should be chosen consonant with this underlying logical premise, because as soon as some other procedural difference is introduced, the contrast that justified the study in the first place is weakened.

In experimental research the term *confounding* is used to describe this type of situation in which some procedural move results in something other than the experimental intervention being done to one group and not the other(s). The random assignment of subjects to groups can be visualized as a strategy specifically implemented to avoid one type of confound—namely the assignment of nonequivalent subjects to groups. Unfortunately, there are many other types of confounds that can influence subjects' ultimate scores on the outcome variable. These artifacts are especially problematic if they are allowed to operate differentially with respect to the experimental groups, because they thereby masquerade as treatment effects (or conspire to mask them). If anything, this is even more problematic in quasi-experimental designs employing intact groups, since the settings associated with these groups often have decided confounds built into them.

It is therefore essential that, once the basic procedural blueprint for the study has been drafted, you take the time to examine each element employed therein for the presence of a possible confound. Thus, for example, if the experimental interventions must be administered to individuals by different experimenters, it could be quite problematic to the study's ultimate validity to confound potential experimenter differences with the treatment groups by having some experimenters work only with the subjects in the intervention group and others work only with those in the control group. Similarly, one would not want subjects in one group to be run in the morning and those in the other groups in the afternoon. One would also not want subjects in one group to be influenced by the experimenter's expectations that the intervention was efficacious (or by his or her negative opinions, based upon knowledge of which subjects were in the control group). In short, nothing should vary between experimental groups except the experimental treatments themselves, and this includes both procedural moves (e.g., one would not administer an extra test, such as a pretest, to one group and not the other) and affective factors (e.g., one would not want to implant any sort of differential expectations or motivations among the groups involved).

The best way to avoid all types of procedural confounds is therefore via a microscopic examination of every element in the study's design, with the objective of discovering any nonexperimental between-group differences in the way subjects are treated. The best way to avoid the types of affective confounds that occur during the course of the study (as well as procedural ones that may be unconsciously implemented by the experimenters) is to employ every ethical means possible to mask group membership from both the subjects and the experimenter(s) themselves. (In medical research this is the primary function of the *double-blind, placebo design.*) When this is not feasible, serious attempts should be made both to make the differences between the groups as unobtrusive as possible and to equate subjects' between-group commitments/expectations. To accomplish these goals it is often necessary—within the confines of common sense and ethical guidelines—to mask the true intentions of the study from the participants, which in turn sometimes necessitates requiring the control group to perform basically irrelevant tasks to disguise its identity and purpose.

It is probably not possible to design a study involving human subjects in such a way that absolutely no irrelevant nontreatment group differences exist. Thus most researchers wouldn't worry that much if two experimental conditions had to be run in two separate rooms—if the environments of these rooms were generally equivalent. (A careful researcher would still investigate the situation, however, making sure that, say, workmen weren't in the process of tearing down a wall adjacent to one and not the other, or that one had a severe heating problem of some sort.)

Suffice it to say that experimental confounds are capable of fatally flawing otherwise well-designed studies if they are not recognized and corrected at the design stage. I would argue, in fact, that one of the primary distinctions between good and bad researchers is therefore the ability:

a. to identify what the experimental confounds in a study are,
b. to recognize which are most threatening to a particular study's validity, and

   c. to compensate for them in some way.

Accomplishing these tasks basically entails sitting down and thinking very carefully about the study and how it will actually be carried out. One profitable way of doing this is to run through every procedural element of the study mentally, as though it were actually being carried out. (Later I will suggest that a research schedule/diary be constructed for implementation of the design, so it might be a good idea to use this tool to identify confounds as well.) Thus, beginning with the assignment of subjects to groups and ending with the collection of the last piece of data from the subjects so assigned, the researcher should attempt to visualize the process as it will actually occur in the experimental setting, with an eye toward identifying things and procedures that will be per-formed for one treatment group but not the other. Each identified procedure should be written down, because the list will be surprisingly long (e.g., slightly different instructions may be necessitated for one group than the other).

Once recognized and listed, the potential effect of each experimental confound should be carefully considered, with respect to its possible role in producing both false positive and false negative results. Two criteria should be used: common sense and how likely the confounding variable is to be related to the outcome variable, as determined by its empirical literature.

Both criteria involve an unavoidable degree of subjectivity, hence the best approach is to design the confound out of the study. When this is not feasible, a formal argument should be prepared that is designed to convince one's worst professional enemy/critic that the confounding variable is not strongly enough related to the outcome variable to constitute a serious alternative explanation for whatever results may eventually accrue.

When a confound is unavoidable, the researcher should, at the very least, make every effort to ameliorate its potential effect. In some cases this can be accomplished procedurally. In others, Principles 19, 20, and 21 probably offer the next best solutions:

▼

Principle 19: **Randomly assign as many of a study's procedural components as possible.**

▼

Deciding which subjects will receive which experimental treatments is not the only profitable use of random assignment. Sometimes, for example, subjects must be run in small groups within each of the experimental treatments. Sometimes these smaller groups must in turn be administered by different experimenters. Alternately, some designs call for the same subjects to receive more than one treatment, and some types of observational measurements require a sampling procedure because it is impossible to record all of the behaviors that may occur during the experimental interval.

All of these design components have one thing in common: They require a selection decision of some sort, which in turn entails the possibility of systematic bias sneaking into the process. While this is often not as serious as the biased assignment of subjects to treatment groups, there is always cause for concern any time the possibility of a systematic selection artifact is allowed to enter the experimental protocol.

Thus, if multiple experimenters are to be used in a study, it is always wiser to randomly assign subjects to experimenters than it is to allow either party to select the other on a nonrandom basis. If subjects must be grouped together within an experimental condition, then it is better to randomly assign them to these subgroups than to permit them to select who they want to interact with. If observational units must be selected, then the selection process should be done on a random basis of some sort. It is most important that the researcher should never allow himself or herself to make arbitrary selection decisions. (In other words, when in doubt—randomize.)

▼

Principle 20: **In addition to randomly assigning procedural elements within the design, always counterbalance these components with respect to the treatments.**

As important as Principle 19 is, it is not always sufficient to avoid the untoward effects of an experimental confound. In the absence of some compelling logical reason, every possible source of systematic variance that is not part of the experimental manipulation should be procedurally spread across treatment groups to the maximum degree possible.

Thus, for example, if two experimenters were employed, one should not administer only the experimental treatment while the other runs only control subjects. Both should administer both experimental and control treatments unless there is some compelling methodological reason why this is not feasible (such as when treatment contamination under such conditions is completely unavoidable). Should the latter be the case, then at a minimum both experimenters should be as blind as possible to the study purpose and have no stake in the study outcome.

Similarly, in a crossover design where each subject is to receive each of two experimental treatments, one would never allow, say, everyone in the study to receive Treatment A first followed by Treatment B. This would completely confound order (and any possible carryover effects) with the treatment comparison and almost surely be fatal to the study's credibility. (It would also do no good to randomly decide which treatment all of the subjects should be exposed to first since order/carryover effects would still be confounded.) Instead, the researcher should randomly select half of the sample to receive Treatment A first, followed by Treatment B. The other half would be assigned by default to receive Treatment B first, followed by Treatment A.

This strategy (as well as the scenario in which multiple experimenters run all treatment groups) is an example of the concept of *counterbalancing*. Its primary purpose is to avoid confounding the source of systematic variation the researcher is interested in studying (i.e., the difference between treatments) with any other source of extraneous variation.

All things being equal, the counterbalancing advice in Principle 20 is more important than the random assignment component of Principle 19. Suppose, for example, that an innovative way of delivering group therapy were being compared with a more traditional modality. Such a contrast would be completely invalidated if one therapist was allowed to administer all of the experimental sessions and another therapist was assigned to all of the traditional ones. No one could ever be sure that the results would not be due to therapist differences rather than to the type of therapy administered. The fact that patients may have been randomly assigned to the two groups would be irrelevant; whether positive or negative results were obtained would also be irrelevant. (For example, a superiority on the part of the experimental condition could be due to the possibility that the therapist assigned to it was superior; no significant differences between the two conditions could mean that the therapist assigned to the traditional modality was so superior that he or she compensated for a potentially inferior treatment.) Furthermore, even randomly assigning one of the therapists to the experimental condition and the other to the comparison group would also be irrelevant, because a significant difference between the two therapists would by necessity produce one of the false positive/false negative scenarios just posited.

It is hoped that this discussion has made the following points:

> As powerful and elegant as random assignment of subjects to treatments is, it is completely impotent in the face of confounding variables. Confounding variables, on the other hand, can usually be perfectly controlled by counterbalancing them with respect to the treatment groups employed.

When counterbalancing is itself either impossible or contraindicated, there is fortunately one final design strategy left to deal with the potentially deleterious effects of experimental confounds:

▼

Principle 21: **When counterbalancing is not feasible, employ a nesting design of some sort.**

▼

As an illustration, suppose that a behavioral scientist was interested in implementing an intricate token reinforcement system in order to reduce disruptive behaviors among socially and emotionally disturbed adolescents. Suppose further that he or she gained access to a special school serving such children, that it was possible to randomly assign students to treatments, but that it was not physically possible to have each teacher teach students, employing both treatments. The study could probably still be performed adequately under certain conditions.

If, for example, only two teachers were to be employed, it might still be possible to work out some sort of counterbalancing scheme, since there are many different forms thereof. One possibility would be to randomly assign this one teacher to teach the experimental group for half of the experimental interval and then to switch over and teach the control condition during the second half (obviously, the second teacher would do the opposite). Here the potential teacher difference variable is not confounded with the treatments. Teacher effects are confounded with order, but this is something that most researchers could live with as long as steps were taken to avoid experimental contamination (e.g., it would be important to ensure that the teacher who used the innovative reinforcement system first did not carry over any of its components when he or she switched classes).

If there is simply not enough flexibility to allow for any form of counterbalancing, the study could still be run if multiple teachers could be employed. If, for example, 20 teachers could be employed in the study, 10 could be randomly assigned to employ the reinforcement intervention, with the other 10 teaching without it. In this scenario, teacher differences would still be confounded with the treatments, but it is so unlikely that all the good ones would be assigned by chance to one and only one of the treatments that the research community would undoubtedly accept the results if the rest of study were well designed.

This particular strategy is called *nesting*, since one of the design components is "nested" or confounded within another. When the nested components can be randomly assigned, and when they are relatively numerous, this particular design is considered quite sound. Another advantage inherent in this design is that the nested variable's relationship with the outcome variable can be both estimated and partialled out from the experimental effect during data analysis.

There are as many forms of nesting as there are of counterbalancing; hence it is impossible to say that one design genre is categorically superior to the other without considering the specific research situation involved. It is safe to say that under the proper conditions, both nesting and counterbalancing procedures can be viable research options. Both should therefore be considered and contrasted when treatment confounds cannot be eliminated from a design via simple random assignment. Generalized, this piece of advice logically produces Principle 22:

▼

Principle 22: **Regardless of the design chosen, consider all the possible alternative explanations for all the possible results that may accrue from it prior to conducting the study.**

▼

In experimental research, this task is facilitated by the fact that there are only two possible erroneous outcomes: false positive and false negative results. (Actually, the obtained results could misrepresent the size of a true positive effect due to imprecision in the study design, but this genre of error is seldom considered that pernicious.) Since these two types of error are equally injurious, I will list a series of questions surrounding a number of different genres of experimental artifacts that need to be answered in order to avoid both false positive and false negative results in experimental studies.

Not all of these artifacts are relevant to all types of experimental studies. Furthermore, the random assignment of subjects, the use of truly meaningful outcome variables, and the application of a bit of common sense in the design process are usually enough to avoid most of them. *Any researcher who opts to employ a quasi-experimental design, however, should be especially vigilant against these artifacts.*

Regardless of the design employed, however, I still think it is a good idea to formally address each of the following eight questions when designing an experiment. If nothing else, this process should help persuade the still unconvinced of the advantages of randomly assigning subjects to both an intervention and a comparison group. Without further ado, then, the eight artifacts and their companion questions are:

Artifact 1: Experimental Confounds. Can anything be identified that is perfectly confounded with the experimental treatments?

Although this has just been discussed in some detail, it is difficult to overemphasize the importance of identifying and eliminating experimental confounds from the research enterprise. The identification, elimination, or debilitation of experimental confounds is so important that this step should always be the first consideration in choosing and refining a study's design. The use of an intact group by definition introduces one type of confound (i.e., any difference, known or unknown, that exists between the groups, their settings, their histories, their members, or the way in which their members were selected into them).

Artifact 2: Selection. Could the subjects in one of the experimental groups possess a greater inborn propensity to change on the outcome variable than the other?

The avoidance of this artifact, also called *selection*, is the crowning achievement of random assignment. In my opinion it is the most common and the most serious of all the possible alternative explanations for research results. When operative, it leads to false positive results when the initial disparity favors the intervention, and false negative results when the opposite occurs.

This particular artifact is especially troublesome because it is difficult to test directly. Even the random assignment of subjects does not provide an absolute guarantee against its occurrence since anything can happen as a function of chance. Random assignment does make differential selection so unlikely, however (especially when reasonably large sample sizes are employed), that it will not be advanced as an alternative explanation by knowledgeable research critics. It will almost always be advanced as a reason not to believe quasi-experimental results, however.

Artifact 3: History. Can the results be influenced by external events, other than the intervention, that occur during the course of the study?

This type of artifact, sometimes called *history*, can be especially troublesome in loosely controlled research involving nonrandomly assigned intact groups. Suppose, for example, that a gerontologist wanted to study the effects of introducing pets into the nursing home environment upon the self-reported quality of life of elderly patients.

The easiest way to do this study might be to gain permission from the director of one home to bring in pets during a certain period of the day and then compare the resultant effects with residents living in a second home that did not offer this service. Such a strategy tempts fate in the sense that it is always possible that something will happen in one of the nursing homes (e.g., the introduction of a different service or an especially demoralizing death) that does not occur in the other. Should this happen, it can produce either false positive or false negative results, depending upon the location of the artifact. Perhaps an equally pernicious factor is that one can never be completely sure that no such invalidating artifacts do occur when employing weak designs, hence the stricture against them.

As with differential selection, history should be guarded against, even under optimal experimental conditions. By far and away the best way to prevent the occurrence of an extraneous event during the course of a study is (a) to keep the experimental interval as short as is conducive with study objectives (the longer the study, the more time there is for something to go wrong) and (b) to stay very close to the experimental setting in order to very carefully monitor what goes on.

The presence of a research diary can also prove quite helpful in documenting the potential existence of this artifact. Regardless of how good a researcher's memory is, it is always a good idea to record exactly what happens and when it occurs during the course of a study. (To be maximally useful, these should be made and dated each day.) Furthermore, everything that occurs should be recorded, regardless of whether it seems relevant at the time or whether the researcher is sure that it will be remembered. If nothing else, it is often helpful when writing the final research report to be able to say exactly when something occurred or when something was done within the experimental interval.

Artifact 4: Maturation. Would the subjects employed be expected to change during the course of the study as a function of time alone?

This is probably more often the case than not. Children mature, patients get better or worse (depending upon the disease state involved), students learn as a function of their everyday curriculum, and the elderly become more frail. In the presence of random assignment, this artifact is problematic only in the sense that the intervention must be strong enough (or the outcome measures used to assess it must be sensitive enough) to register an effect over and above this natural tendency for change.

In many ways, the maturation concept is similar to the differential selection artifact. Unlike selection, however, "maturing" or "naturally changing" subjects are not something that should be necessarily avoided because it is often this very tendency that the researcher wishes to speed up (e.g., learning in the schooling paradigm) or slow down (e.g., the debilitating effects of a chronic disease). The existence of this phenomenon is extremely problematic, however, in something like a one-group, pretest/posttest design because the subjects would be expected to change as a function of time alone. Maturation as a potential alternative explanation is, in fact, the primary reason why this design is held in such poor regard within the research community and why, in my opinion, it should not even be considered by anyone wishing to conduct meaningful empirical research.

Artifact 5: Regression Toward the Mean. Were the subjects chosen because they exhibited more extreme scores on the outcome variable, or because they exhibited a greater need for the experimental intervention?

A positive answer to this question is also quite likely, since it is not at all usual to select subjects because they exhibited either high or low scores on an outcome variable. Medical research, for example, usually involves subjects with physiological symptoms that need reduction. It is also not uncommon in many other types of research to exclude subjects who do not need an intervention or who score near the ceiling of the proposed outcome variable. (This will even be suggested in the next chapter as a means of increasing a study's statistical power.)

While often a recommended strategy, employing only subjects who exhibit extreme scores on the outcome variable does produce a purely statistical artifact called *regression toward the mean*. Unlike the other artifacts discussed above, this one is somewhat outside the realm of common sense, and many of its implications are poorly understood, even among experienced researchers.

It operates as follows: Every variable, by definition of the term, possesses a distribution within the general population, whereby some people possess high scores and some people possess low scores. This is true whether we are talking about standardized test scores, personality factors, intelligence, height, weight, blood pressure, or white cell counts. For those measures possessing the possibility of any substantive degree of change across time, either as a function of measurement error or as a function of true change due to external forces, a second administration of the test used will result in an interesting phenomenon. Those scores near the top of the distribution the first time around will be slightly lower on the second testing, while the opposite is true for those near the bottom of the distribution.

Although a somewhat difficult concept to grasp, regression toward the mean as an alternative explanation for research results can be very simply avoided by randomly assigning subjects to treatments. When this is done, extreme groups can be profitably employed, because the effect can be assumed to operate equally for all treatments involved. Things aren't quite this simple, however, when a nonrandomly assigned comparison group is employed, since it is always possible that either more or fewer of its subjects may have artifactually exhibited extreme scores at the beginning of the experiment. On the other hand, when a single group design is used with such subjects, this natural tendency to change across time is especially problematic since it can either be mistaken for an intervention effect (i.e., a false positive result) or mask a true one (i.e., produce a false negative result).

Artifact 6: Differential Experimental Mortality. Are subjects in, say, the intervention group more likely to drop out of the study than those in the control group?

The answer to this question carries with it a number of implications. On the simplest level, if substantive attrition is perceived to be likely, it is important to attempt to ascertain whether enough subjects will be left to achieve statistical significance (see Principle 28). For that reason, the general problem of retaining as many subjects as possible in the study will be discussed in the next chapter.

What we are discussing here, however, is the much more problematic scenario, in which more subjects are lost in one treatment than in the other. It can be argued that attrition of subjects during a study is usually little more than a nuisance if it is *not differential*, simply because it can be compensated for by planning the initial sample size to compensate for the subsequent loss of power. From a generalizability viewpoint, it also can be argued that any positive result accruing implies that the intervention is at least capable of working for the types of subjects who have the perseverance to see the experience through. A *differential* subject loss, on the other hand, casts grave doubt on the validity of either a positive or a negative outcome, simply because it is always possible (and probably usually likely) that the subjects who were lost from the study would have scored differently on the final administration of the outcome variable than would subjects who were actually measured.

When differential subject loss (which is sometimes called *differential experimental mortality*) does occur, it is usually assumed to operate in favor of the intervention. This is because the intervention usually requires more of subjects than of simple controls, hence encouraging more of the less conscientious (or busy) subjects to drop out of the former than the latter. When this occurs a very serious, potentially fatal alternative explanation exists for whatever the final results happen to be, so it behooves the researcher to try to limit both differential and nondifferential experimental mortality as much as possible. (It should be noted, however, that differential mortality can favor the control condition, as when the more motivated individuals assigned thereto see that they are not being "helped" and thus seek better treatment elsewhere.)

Differential experimental mortality is probably best avoided by making the experimental treatments as comparable as possible, with respect to (a) the effort required of their subjects and (b) their intrinsic interest. This may, in turn, involve such strategies as jazzing up a control group so that its members do not perceive it to be a completely meaningless activity or even requiring more of them than is really necessary if the intervention is relatively undemanding. (Basically, I would recommend neither of these latter strategies unless pilot work indicated that general experimental mortality was going to be a problem with the types of subjects employed and there appeared to be no way to avoid same.)

Since it is often not possible to know how successful steps such as these are until the study is over, it is wise to design an evaluation of the extent to which differential mortality does or does not occur. This entails collecting relevant information early in the study, so that people who drop out and people who remain can be compared as much as possible. Such a comparison, even if it proves negative, can never definitively "prove" that the accruing results would have been valid if attrition had not occurred, but it may provide some support for such a contention. (It can also sometimes be helpful to contact dropouts and simply ask them why they did not complete the study.)

Artifact 7: Obtrusive Research Procedures. Will the experimental setting be obtrusive enough to encourage subjects to behave atypically?
    This is often a difficult question to answer, partly because there are so many factors that potentially affect the individual's response to an experiment. Undoubtedly the most famous example of atypical experimental behavior came from industrial research conducted in Hawthorne, New York (hence the Hawthorne effect), in which the researchers concluded that the subjects' knowledge that they were being studied (or at least the attention being paid to them) "caused" them to increase their productivity. Obviously, such a phenomenon, if general, would have serious research implications, since individuals who received an intervention often have more contact with research personnel and receive more attention therefrom than do members of control conditions.
    There are many other well-known examples, such as the placebo effect in medicine, whereby the very fact that subjects think they will be helped by a treatment seems to "cause" them to change on a number of outcome variables. Closely related are demand characteristics (i.e., something in the experimental design that encourages the subject to interpret the study purpose and behave accordingly) and related concepts such as the "good subject" phenomenon (whereby subjects attempt to behave the way they think researchers want them to behave).
    There is very little consensus surrounding the extent to which any of these artifacts actually operate to invalidate day-to-day research findings. The Hawthorne effect, for example, seems to be pretty much discredited today, based upon (a) statistical reanalyses of the original data that question whether it ever occurred, and (b) the fact that studies possessing an extra control group designed to document the effect's existence usually fail to do so. Similar controversy and contradictory evidence surrounds the placebo effect, subjects' expectancies, and experimental expectancies as well.
    This inconclusiveness is not atypical in methodological research in general and it is not likely to be resolved anytime soon. I would therefore counsel researchers as follows:

a. *Specifically design experimental interventions and experimental procedures to be as unobtrusive as possible.* Once this is done, do not be overly concerned about subjects' changing their behavior as a sole function of their interpretation of the experimental purposes. I personally have never found subjects to be that cooperative.

b. *In relation to the above, make sure that the various treatments employed are not differentially obtrusive.* One of my more notable experimental failures involved an attempt to assess the effects of increasing teacher knowledge upon student achievement. I randomly assigned teachers (actually undergraduate education majors) to either receive instruction in the topic they were to teach or not receive such instruction. The resulting effect on their pupils' subsequent learning was so large that I became suspicious and formally surveyed both groups as to their motivations regarding the study. What I found was that the experimental teachers reported taking the experience quite seriously, while the noninstructed teachers considered the whole thing to be just another "ridiculous" experiment. Some of the latter even reported not teaching the experimental topic when no one was around to observe them.

c. *Volunteer as little information as possible about a study's expected outcomes.* The solicitation of informed consent usually does not require that a study's hypotheses and experimental design be explained in any detail, only that the subjects be told what may be required of them and what the potential personal effects/implications of these requirements are. This means that it is perfectly permissible to "blind" both the subject and the experimenter with respect to group assignment.

d. *Be very aware of the many roles that your personal bias can play in the design, conduct, analysis, and interpretation of experimental research.* Standardize all experimental procedures (e.g., when possible, use prewritten scripts) as much as possible to reduce this potentially debilitating factor. Also, standardize all interactions with subjects to the maximum degree possible. For data that require some sort of scoring decisions, always blind the scorer with respect to group membership.

e. *When there is doubt about experimental obtrusiveness and/or bias, anonymously survey the participating parties after the study is over.* A number of investigators have used this strategy to demonstrate that even subjects in studies employing placebos can often guess the treatment to which they have been assigned. My above-mentioned experiences in this regard have led me to suggest that subjects always be surveyed following an experiment, to ascertain the degree to which any suspected artifacts may have been operating.

Artifact 8: Reactive Outcome Measures. Is the outcome variable, or the manner in which it is administered, sufficiently obtrusive to make subjects behave atypically?

Sometimes the most obtrusive, reactive, and obvious part of a study is its outcome variable. Such problems are confounded by an interesting phenomenon endemic to most paper-and-pencil and performance type measures: Everything else being equal, *people usually score higher (or more appropriately) on a test the second time they take it, even when no formal intervention occurs between the first and the second administrations.* This is often true of both cognitive and affective measures. It probably occurs because people remember errors they made the first time around and/or are more experienced with the items themselves, hence are able to respond more appropriately.

The implications of this measurement artifact (called *testing* by some methodologists) are obvious. In weak designs such as single-group, pretest/posttest designs, subjects are likely to improve from pretest to posttest irrespective of any experimental treatment, hence resulting in false positive findings.

This artifact has at least theoretically possible implications for true experimental designs as well, since it is possible that the intervention will be more likely to cause subjects to "pay more attention" to the outcome variable, hence making the testing artifact operate differentially. Alternately, the pretest (or even the act of being pretested) could potentially sensitize subjects to the intervention. There is little empirical evidence, however, that this latter artifact (sometimes called *pretest sensitization*) does operate differentially in day-to-day research. Still, it is always a good practice to decrease a study's obtrusiveness whenever possible, hence the following recommendations:

a. *Do not employ excessively obvious variables in the first place*, such as "attitudes toward this-or-that," followed by an intervention designed to alert subjects to what their "attitudes toward this-or-that" ought to be. It can be argued that variables such as this are seldom that important anyway.

b. *Do not employ pretests in studies that must use such "obvious" measures.* Pretests are not necessary when subjects are randomly assigned to groups, since it can be assumed that no pre-experimental differences will exist between groups anyway. Pretests do increase statistical power, but other controlling variables (see Principle 27) can usually be identified that function almost as well. The situation is complicated for quasi-experimental designs that depend much more heavily upon statistical control. Here it may not be possible to identify anything other than an identical pretest that will correlate highly enough with the outcome variable.

(I personally do not recommend the two most common procedural strategies for dealing with this artifact: the Solomon four-group design and the use of retrospective pretests. The former is wasteful with respect to statistical power, and the latter's validity remains to be demonstrated. In my opinion, the best approach is simply to attempt to reduce the obtrusiveness of both one's intervention and outcome variables.)

Artifact 9: Experimental Contamination. Will the design permit cross-contamination of subjects?

Cross-contamination occurs when experimental subjects have the opportunity of communicating the essence of the intervention to their control counterparts, hence theoretically resulting in a false negative result. In my opinion this is an alternative explanation that is worried about considerably more than it should be. Most interventions are far too complex to transfer so easily, and few subjects are conscientious (or interested) enough to spend their free time attempting to reenact same. There is some evidence, however, that subjects will talk about a study, even when requested not to; hence, simply asking subjects not to discuss experimental procedures with anyone may not be especially effective.

Should cross-contamination therefore appear potentially problematic, the likelihood of its occurrence can be reduced by:

a. not assigning close dyads (e.g., roommates or spouses) to separate treatments,
b. revealing as little about the research design and purposes as possible,
c. keeping the experimental interval as brief as possible,
d. avoiding the prolonged use of facilities in which subjects in one group routinely interact with subjects in the other, and
e. asking subjects not to discuss the experimental procedure with anyone else (because some at least will comply).

My later recommendations (Principle 33) regarding the use of a post-intervention questionnaire can also be applied to ascertain the effect to which experimental contamination may have occurred. If some contamination is reported, and if the questionnaires were not anonymous, the data can be analyzed, both including and excluding the offending subjects, to ascertain the seriousness of the problem.

It is hoped that the very act of considering each of the nine questions above will facilitate the prevention of these artifacts. Should the answer to one of these questions be an unqualified "yes," and no practical way around the problem can be found, I would advise the selection of another hypothesis to test. It has been my experience, however, that most problems identified at the design stage of a study can be solved with a little creativity and perhaps a little help from a more experienced colleague.

Suggested Readings

I am personally aware of more than 75 research methodology textbooks, most of which are adequate for giving students a general overview of experimental design but are inadequate for actually helping them conduct an experiment. Certainly, every prospective researcher should study at least one of these texts conscientiously. Usually choice is dictated by whatever is required in one's primary doctoral research methods course. In the event that you have the liberty to choose your own, one possibility might be:

Pedhazur, E. J., & Schmelkin, L. P. (1991). *Measurement, design, and analysis: An integrated approach*. Hillsdale, NJ: Lawrence Erlbaum.

References that can be quite helpful in the actual design process itself are:

Bausell, R. B. (1986). *A practical guide to conducting empirical research*. New York: Harper & Row.
    Modesty prevents too lavish a recommendation of this book, but it was written as an attempt to make all the major design, measurement, and statistical concepts deemed important in the day-to-day conduct of empirical research accessible to practicing researchers.

Campbell, D. T., & Stanley, J. C. (1966). *Experimental and quasi-experimental designs for research*. Chicago: Rand McNally.

> This is *the* modern experimental design classic. It contains only 71 pages but has absolutely no fat and probably contains more content pertinent to experimental design than most texts 10 times its length. (It might also be noted that the majority of such texts in the social, behavioral, and health sciences borrow heavily from the concepts and terminology presented in this little book.)

Cook, T. D., & Campbell, D. (1979). *Quasi-experimentation: Design and analysis issues in field settings*. Boston: Houghton-Mifflin.

> This book, like the one by Campbell and Stanley (1966), has also become a classic. I would recommend that anyone contemplating the conduct of a quasi-experimental read it prior to doing so.

6

Designing Experimental Studies to Achieve Statistical Significance

The previous chapter was dedicated to avoiding results due to factors extraneous to the experimental intervention(s) being tested. As we discussed, such erroneous results may be in the form of either:

1. false positive results (e.g., the intervention may have been completely ineffective, but more subjects with poor prognoses dropped out of the experimental group, thus making it look beneficial) or

2. false negative results (e.g., the intervention may have been quite beneficial, but poor prognosis subjects dropped out of the control group, thus inflating its overall mean and thereby masking the true experimental effect).

There is one genre of error, however, that can be problematic even in studies that follow all the advice presented up to this point. This type of error surrounds one specialized form of false negative result:

Failing to reject the null hypothesis (or at least failing to adequately test it) because the study design is not sensitive enough to document a truly effective intervention.

The present chapter is therefore dedicated solely to avoiding this particular scenario. I ascribe so much importance to it for two reasons. First, the design strategies that must be instituted in order to provide a sensitive hypothesis test also usually help avoid many of the types of errors discussed in Chapter 5. Second, with the notable exception of Mark Lipsey's absolutely wonderful book, *Design Sensitivity: Statistical Power for Experimental Research* (Sage Publications, 1990), few research methodology texts (which is the primary medium for training social, behavioral, and health scientists) emphasize the following fact:

> It takes a considerable amount of skill to design and conduct research sensitive enough to document the existence of a true effect within the stylized confines of an empirical research study. Most of the things that are likely to go wrong with a study (at least one in which random assignment of subjects to treatments is employed) conspire to prohibit the documentation of a true effect, rather than artifactually producing spurious positive results.

The keyword here is *sensitivity*. In many ways a research design is an observational instrument, similar to a microscope or a telescope, except that the view it affords us is always relatively distorted. Instead of a lens, a research study provides us with a model for viewing reality. Thus, even under the best of circumstances, the representation provided by this model is only an approximation of the real world. It affords us only an estimate of the true parameters surrounding the phenomena we are interested in studying, because every element comprised in the model (e.g., the subjects we feed into it, the procedures we design for them, and the observations we perform upon them) contributes a certain amount of distortion. If extreme care is not therefore exercised in the construction of each of these components, then there is no way that we will be able to observe anything with sufficient precision to permit us to make a reliable inference from our model to the reality to which we aspire.

Without further ado, then, allow me to offer what is perhaps the second most important design principle of conducting experimental research (Principle 17 remains in first place):

▼

Principle 23: **Design empirical research, first and foremost, to obtain statistically significant differences among your experimental groups.**

▼

The wholehearted adoption of Principle 23 does not imply foregoing any degree of objectivity or honesty, only that you as a researcher perceive the primary purpose of your design efforts to be the achievement of statistical significance by every available legitimate means possible. (The achievement of statistical significance, it will be remembered, implies the acceptance of your hypothesis, which is the accepted means by which an inference is allowed from the model, represented by the research design, to the real world.) Scientific progress is measured primarily by positive results, not negative ones. None of us would recognize Jonas Salk's name if the huge clinical trial evaluating his vaccine (the intervention) had not been designed with an eye toward legitimately achieving a statistical significant decreased incidence of polio (the outcome).

Most of the discussion and resulting advice that follow, therefore, will be offered in terms of enhancing the likelihood of producing a study sensitive enough to document a positive result, should one truly exist. The primary purpose for all the decisions regarding a study's design, in fact, can be conceptualized as directly impacting upon this all-important sensitivity issue. Since the easiest way of ensuring that we can observe something through a flawed instrument is to look for a large object rather than a small one, the first genre of design issues that will be discussed revolves around attempting to maximize the size of the effect that we are trying to simulate via our experimental design. Only after taking this step will we consider means of increasing the observational power of the instrument itself.

▼

Principle 24: **When applied and theoretical considerations permit, design the intervention(s) to maximize the differences between groups (i.e., the effect size) by employing only subjects who are likely to profit from the intervention.**

This is a direct corollary of Principle 23 because, everything else being equal, the greater the absolute difference between the groups involved, the more likely the null hypothesis is to be rejected. The most direct means of obtaining such a difference is to define the treatment(s) and comparison group(s) in such a way that they will be as different

from one another as possible, within the constraints of scientific meaningfulness, and to exclude subjects who do not need the intervention
being tested.

Suppose, for example, that an educational researcher wished to study
the effects of increasing the length of classroom instructional periods
for elementary school children. To begin with, there is no question that
our researcher would be absolutely assured of rejecting a null hypothesis
involving a comparison between 60-minute and, say, 10-minute class
periods. Such a comparison would certainly "maximize the difference
between groups," but any findings accruing therefrom would hold no
interest to anyone in education, since no school anywhere (hopefully)
devotes only 10 minutes to the instruction of basic curricular topics. In
the same vein, our researcher would not want to contrast 60 minutes of
instruction to a pure control group receiving no instruction at all,
because such a study, although assured of rejecting the null hypothesis,
would simply assess whether children learned as a function of instruction, not if longer class periods were more effective than shorter ones.

Needless to say, it is not always so obvious what constitutes a meaningful difference between groups in real-world research. Being able to make
determinations such as this is one of the primary mandates for knowing
one's discipline (Principle 6) and for knowing its research literature
(Principle 8). It is here, and within that rare and nebulous attribute called
common sense, that the true definition of "meaningful differences" lies.

Although the way in which the experimental groups are constructed
has the most obvious impact upon maximizing the study's likely effect
size, it is by no means the only parameter involved. Other means of
increasing an effect size include:

*1. Making sure that the experimental interval is long enough to allow
an effect to manifest itself (but not long enough for subjects in all the
groups involved to approach a ceiling score on the outcome variable
employed).* As will be discussed later, the determination of an optimal
experimental interval is one of the primary functions of a pilot study
(Principle 30). Also, there is somewhat of a trade-off here with respect
to avoiding experimental contamination, since the longer a study runs,
the more likely something is to go wrong with it (e.g., experimental
mortality). Still, the main criterion for determining how long the experimental interval lasts should be maximization of the intervention
versus control contrast.

2. Employing as few treatment groups as possible (two are optimal). Since research subjects are normally in short supply, the use of multiple treatments results in fewer available subjects within each group. This in turn reduces the probability of obtaining statistically significant differences. Even when subjects are not limited, however, more subjects per treatment are needed for these studies, since the study's alpha level must be protected for the multiple contrasts such studies require. In the presence of limited resources, then, I would always counsel beginning with a two-group design.

3. As a corollary of 2, I would argue that, as a first research priority, it is usually better to find a treatment that works than it is to be able to definitively explain why it works. Thus I would recommend constructing a single powerful treatment group and contrasting it to a single meaningful comparison group, even if this means that you won't know exactly which constituent or combination of constituents was most responsible for the statistically significant effect obtained. I realize that there is a certain amount of scientific prejudice against this "black box" approach, as it is called by its critics, but it is certainly clinically defensible in areas that currently lack effective interventions.

This advice, however, must be weighed with respect to its potential advantage (i.e., increased statistical power) and its considerable disadvantage (lack of scientific clarity). One of the primary strengths of experimental research resides in its ability to tease out specific causal agents and to refine theory; thus, if resources permit, it is foolish not to avail yourself of this potential.

In designing a program to enable overweight cardiac bypass patients to lose weight after surgery, for example, a researcher might determine (from pilot work, previous research, or theory) that the most effective technique would involve a combination of dietary training and supervised exercise. If his or her subject pool were restricted, then I would suggest a combined intervention versus treatment-as-usual comparison group in order to ensure sufficient statistical power. The problem with such a strategy, however, would be that if statistical significance were achieved, our researcher would know only that the combination of dietary instruction and exercise worked, not which was the more important element, and not even that both were essential. If sufficient subjects were available, on the other hand, the researcher could add two more intervention groups to his or her design: exercise only and dietary instruction only. Then, the three intervention groups could be compared to one another to see (a) if the combined program was superior to dietary instruction and exercise alone, and (b) if one of these latter programs was superior to the other. Obviously, any scientist would prefer the superior explanatory power of this latter design, but most would also prefer statistical significance between two groups to nonstatistically significant differences among four. What I would advise, therefore, is that you try to conduct your research in settings where the availability of subjects is not problematic.

4. Employing those subjects that are most likely to profit from the intervention (again within practical and theoretical limits). In a study designed to induce people to vote in an upcoming election, for example, it would be quite reasonable for a political scientist to exclude from his or her sample anyone who had a consistently good voting record prior to the random assignment process. Similarly, in a study designed to reduce high-risk sexual behaviors, the researcher would employ only sexually active individuals who did not engage in safe sexual practices. To include individuals who do not need the intervention being tested is wasteful of resources and results in a dilution of the final intervention versus control differences.

Subjects' initial scores on the outcome variable do not constitute the only reason for excluding them from a study. It would be patently foolish, for example, to employ any subjects who were unlikely to profit from an intervention or who were likely to change on the outcome variable for reasons other than the intervention. Thus, in our weight-loss study involving cardiac bypass patients, not only would we obviously exclude patients who were not overweight, but we would also probably exclude any patients who:

a. did not speak English and hence could not understand our instructions or fill out our questionnaires, or
b. were on any kind of medications that precluded them from exercising, affected their attention span, or gave them an independent tendency to either lose or gain weight (including retaining water).

Deciding upon exclusion criteria for one's subjects is one of the most crucial set of decisions a researcher must make in the design of his or her research. They must be set prior to the introduction of the intervention (e.g., one does not exclude subjects who do not profit from same after the fact) and they must have a sound theoretical rationale. They should also be used sparingly because they (a) limit the numbers of subjects available and (b) limit the extent to which one's findings can be generalized (e.g., if we exclude, say, subjects over age 65 from our study, then we cannot assume that an even wildly successful intervention will work for elderly people).

5. Employing a no-treatment control group when ethically and theoretically feasible. Half of any intervention versus control/comparison group effect size resides in the way in which the latter is defined. Hence, deflating the strength of the comparison group is as effective from a statistical perspective as inflating the strength of the experimental group. A pure control that receives no treatment will almost always score lower on the outcome variable than a treatment-as-usual control group. Pure control groups are, of course, recommended only when they make conceptual sense, such as when no effective treatment is known or when a pure control has intrinsic theoretical interest. Still, there are plenty of occasions when a pure control group is useful, and you should certainly never go out of your way to add anything to your comparison group(s) that is not necessary for scientific or clinical meaningfulness.

▼

Principle 25: **Always employ outcome measures that are both reliable and sensitive to change.**

The underlying principle surrounding Principle 23 resides in maximizing the differences among groups that can be explained by the experimental manipulation while at the same time minimizing those differences within groups that cannot be explained. One prime contributor to differences in subjects' scores that cannot be explained is unreliability in the measure chosen to represent the outcome. It therefore behooves the researcher to select those measures that are as precise and error-free as possible. For multiple-item instruments, this is usually easily checked prior to running the study by trying the measure out on a sample of 30 or 40 subjects and computing a coefficient alpha on the results. For single-item instruments, it is best checked by a test-retest procedure or (as in the case for physiologically oriented instruments) by ensuring that the instrumentation itself is properly calibrated and the people who are using it are doing so properly.

The stability (i.e., reliability) with which a measure assigns scores to individuals, however, is only a rudimentary first step in the process of selecting a research instrument. Most researchers will have no difficulty in finding a measure with a reliability coefficient of .80 or better. Far more important is the second part of Principle 25, since *it does absolutely no good to select or construct a perfectly reliable outcome measure that is not sensitive enough to detect intervention-induced changes within the sample employed.* As will be discussed in the next chapter, the best way to ensure the availability of such measures is to select them specifically for this purpose and tailor them (if necessary) specifically for the types of subjects you plan to employ in your study.

Principle 26: **Whenever possible, employ dependent variables that are directly rather than indirectly manipulable by the independent variable.**

Epistemologically, an experiment is conducted to demonstrate a causal link between an independent variable and a dependent variable. If a second variable intervenes between this link (i.e., the intervention must first effect the mediating variable, which in turn causes the dependent variable of interest to change), then the study's overall statistical power is rather dramatically reduced.

In a study designed to see if a behavioral modification program could induce lower consumption of cholesterol and fatty acids, for example, one would expect a direct causal link to exist between the presence/absence of the intervention and cholesterol/fat consumption. Serum cholesterol levels should also be affected, but this is one step removed in the causal link (i.e., the behavioral modification intervention causes dietary changes, which cause reduced serum cholesterol levels). Demonstrating an effect upon the latter would not be impossible, but it would be considerably more difficult to do so because less statistical power exists for that purpose. Taking this logic one step further, we would also expect the behavioral modification intervention to have an effect upon heart attacks and stroke, but the number of subjects necessary to demonstrate this type of effect would be far beyond the means of most researchers. Whenever possible, then, proximal rather than distal outcome variables should be employed. (Mark Lipsey's above-mentioned work supplies a very helpful chart to demonstrate just how much the latter is capable of reducing an experiment's statistical power/effect size.)

▼

Principle 27: **Always employ either controlling variables (i.e., covariates), within-subjects factors (i.e., via a randomized block or repeated measures design), or between-subjects grouping variables (e.g., blocking variables) to increase your study's statistical power.**

▼

All of the strategies listed in Principle 27 are means of reducing unexplained error variance. In a two-group study that employs none of these techniques, there are two sources of variations in subjects' scores. The first is variation *between* the groups, which we assume can be explained solely by the procedural differences between said groups (i.e., the intervention versus the control/comparison condition). The second is variation *within* the groups, which we cannot explain (and hence call *unexplained* or *error* variance), because as far as we know, everyone within the groups received the same treatment and should have scored similarly on the outcome variable.

A statistical procedure that employs only a single independent variable (e.g., a *t*-test) simply compares the size (which translates to the mean difference) of a study's explained variance to its unexplained counterpart. If the former is enough larger than the latter, then the results are declared statistically significant. If they are not, then the results are declared nonsignificant.

The existence of additional variables drastically changes this situation, however, if they existed prior to the beginning of the study (and therefore were not capable of being affected by the experimental treatment) and if they are correlated with the dependent variable. This is due to the fact that the very existence of this correlation implies that we can now explain some of this within-group variation, and the extent to which we can (which is directly related to the extent of the correlations involved) is the extent to which we can reduce the study's error variance. Reducing error variance has the same effect as increasing explained variance, which in turn is comparable to increasing the study's effect size.

Thus, returning to our cholesterol reduction example, if subjects (presumably those in need of same) could be rank-ordered on some continuous variable prior to the introduction of the intervention (say, serum cholesterol levels or grams of cholesterol consumed per day), and randomly assigned in matched pairs to receive either the intervention or, say, an attention placebo condition of some sort, the only source of variation in the outcome variable scores that we could not explain would be when two matched individuals did not perform exactly as we predicted they would, based upon the matching mechanism. This design is sometimes called a *randomized block design* and it results in considerably more statistical power than its purely between-subjects counterpart. As an example, if the mean difference accruing from a two-group study employing no such blocking variable had been projected to be approximately one-fifth of the outcome variable's standard deviation (which is called its effect size), almost 400 subjects per group would be required to achieve statistical significance. If the proposed blocking variable were to correlate, say, .80 with the outcome variable, then the effect size for the new design would be effectively increased to approximately one-third of a standard deviation *and the number of subjects required to achieve statistical significance would be reduced from approximately 400 to 161.* In the more usual case, where a moderate effect size was hypothesized (i.e., one-half of a standard deviation), the use of such a covariate would reduce the subject requirements from 64 to 24 per group. (What this design simulates, then, is the situation in which the same subjects receive both treatments—also called a *crossover* or *repeated measures design*—and the analytic procedure for dealing with the two is identical.)

The same basic effect would accrue from using a preexisting variable such as this in an analysis of covariance, although this is a procedurally more simple strategy since it is not necessary to rank subjects prior to the beginning of the experiment. Here all the researcher need do is find a preexisting variable that is related to the dependent variable, record it, and enter it into the computer at the data analytic phase. This particular design strategy is so easy and powerful that the only excuse I can think for not employing it is in situations in which a correlated preexisting variable cannot be located. (Even here the outcome variable can usually be administered as a pretest, which will serve the same function.) Both techniques, then, accomplish two extremely important functions. They operationally increase a study's effect size and they force the two groups to be equivalent on the preexisting variable(s) in question, thereby increasing the experiment's precision.

The final design strategy is somewhat similar. It also requires a preexisting measure that is correlated with the outcome variable, but it differs from both analysis of covariance and the two within-subjects strategies in the sense that it enables the researcher to ascertain whether the intervention is differentially effective for certain types of subjects or for certain types of conditions. It does this by employing a variable to group subjects who are expected to either perform differently from one another on the outcome variable (which is another way of saying that a correlation is expected between the grouping and outcome variables) or react differently from one another to the experimental treatments (which is another way of saying that a treatment × grouping variable interaction is expected). It is optimal that grouping variables are identified prior to the experiment, in which case subjects are randomly assigned independently within each group to treatments. (Examples of such variables might be males versus females, whites versus blacks, patients with prior hospitalizations versus those without, children attending School #1 versus School #2, or individuals with an income of more than $50,000 versus those with incomes of $49,999 or less.) Thus, as discussed in Chapter 5, in any true experimental design, if we wished to study the potential differential effect of an intervention upon some categorical variable (e.g., gender) we could randomly assign half of one sex to the intervention and half to the control. We would then do the same thing to the opposite sex, resulting in equal numbers of males and females within each of the experimental treatments. (When this is not possible, there is nothing wrong with identifying post hoc grouping variables, although this is likely to result in uneven distributions of the different types of subjects within the experimental groups. Obviously, it will also increase the probability of obtaining a false positive result if the experimenter goes on a fishing expedition and keeps trying out possibilities until one that "works" is finally located.)

All the advice tendered so far in this chapter has been dedicated to maximizing the chances of obtaining statistically significant differences among a study's experimental groups. Once you have maximized your intervention versus control expected effect size, selected sensitive outcome measures, and employed at least one preexisting variable to increase the precision of your design, however, *you still have to employ enough subjects to ensure that you can document a statistically sig-*

nificant difference among your groups. Principle 28 offers the most direct means of ascertaining how many subjects are indeed "enough."

▼

Principle 28: **Always conduct a power analysis to ascertain how many subjects must be employed to allow at least an 80% (and preferably 95%) chance of obtaining statistical significance.**

▼

No other design principle is more important than this one in increasing the probability of obtaining statistical significance. Determining how many subjects are actually needed for any given study is a relatively straightforward process once the following four simple decisions are made:

1. Choosing an acceptable level for obtaining false positive results. This decision, which is synonymous with choosing the error of falsely rejecting the null hypothesis (i.e., of obtaining statistical significance when no real differences existed), is really pretty much out of the researcher's hands, unless he or she wishes to adopt an uncustomarily conservative stance. By far and away the most common practice is to adopt the conventional .05 alpha level, which is synonymous with saying that we are willing to be wrong 5 times out of 100 if we achieve statistical significance. (This is also called the probability of committing a Type I error.) Choosing a more stringent level, say .01, substantially increases the number of subjects needed to achieve statistical significance, because we wish to reduce the probability of a false positive error to 1%.

2. Choosing an acceptable level for obtaining false negative results. This decision is completely up to the researcher, although he or she takes a major risk of failing to achieve statistical significance if it is set too high. Conventional wisdom seems to indicate that a .20 chance of this category of error (called Type II error) is acceptable. Some methodologists (of whom I happen to be one) argue that it makes little sense to consider Type II error as more benign than its Type I counterpart, which means that the researcher should set his or her chances of making a Type II error at .05.

3. Choosing the statistical procedure by which the hypothesis will be tested. The type of statistical procedures available for testing a study's hypothesis is primarily dictated by how Principle 27 was implemented. In most cases this will entail an analysis of covariance, a factorial analysis of variance, a within-subjects analysis of variance, or some combination thereof. Regardless of the specific form the analysis in question takes, it is always helpful if a reasonable estimate is available of what the relationship(s) is (are) between the study's outcome variable and its covariate/blocking variable(s), because this value has a major impact upon the study's statistical power.

4. Estimating what the effect size is likely to be. In research involving differences between two treatments, the effect size is defined simply as the mean difference between the two groups involved, divided by the standard deviation. Thus an estimated effect size of 1.0 in a two-group study would mean that we expect our intervention subjects to score one standard deviation (on average) higher than our control subjects. An estimated effect size of 0.5 would mean that we only expected the mean difference to be one-half of a standard deviation. Many beginning researchers are uncomfortable in making this judgment/guess, but hints are usually available from the literature employing similar variables and from one's pilot data. Meta-analyses provide especially good estimates of effect sizes and, interestingly, Mark Lipsey's Herculean analysis of 102 such studies provides good empirical evidence for Jacob Cohen's suggestion of .50 as a reasonable estimate for behavioral research. (Lipsey's grand effect size mean was .45.) Thus, in the absence of better evidence, I would suggest the use of Cohen's originally suggested .50 as a benchmark.

Results of a typical power analysis. Let us assume that the researcher does indeed opt (a) to set his or her Type I error rate at .05, (b) employs a covariate that is estimated to correlate .30 with the study's dependent variable, and (c) wishes to design his or her study so that it will have an 80% chance of rejecting the null hypothesis in the presence of a medium effect size. A perusal of one of the books containing power/sample size tables, for example, Cohen, J. (1988). *Statistical Power Analysis for the Behavioral Sciences*. New York: Academic Press; or Kraemer, H. C., and Thiemann, S. (1987). *How Many Subjects?* Newbury Park, CA: Sage, would correspondingly indicate a need for 58 subjects per group, although it should be kept in mind that power analyses result in estimates only. To be safe, therefore, it is wise to employ as many subjects as possible within reasonable limits. (*Reasonableness* might be defined as using enough subjects to obtain a 95% chance of rejecting the null hypothesis.) When economic and practical constraints conspire to limit the availability of subjects, I strongly suggest that the researcher consider the following underutilized option when conditions warrant:

▼

Principle 29: **If intervention subjects are considerably more difficult (or expensive) to run than control subjects, increase your sample size by randomly assigning up to three times as many subjects to the latter as to the former.**

▼

This can be a very powerful strategy if one of the conditions is cheaper or less demanding to run (such as a treatment-as-usual group). It will increase the available statistical power dramatically, although the efficiency of the procedure begins to drop off after a 3:1 ratio has been achieved.

Summary

This chapter was basically designed around Principle 23 (design empirical research, first and foremost, to accept your research hypothesis). This simple piece of advice constitutes the cornerstone of my approach to (and philosophy of) experimental design and could just as easily be restated in the following alternative principle: *Build as much statistical power into your research design as possible.*

Since this concept is so central to the conduct of experimental research, the strategies for achieving it probably deserve to be summarized. In way of review, then, the most direct means of increasing a study's statistical power are to:

1. Maximize the effect size by:
    a. Employing the most powerful intervention that is scientifically meaningful.
    b. Employing as few treatment groups as possible (two is optimal).

    c. Monitoring the implementation of both experimental and control conditions carefully over the course of the study.

    d. Employing a no-treatment or pure control group if scientifically meaningful. If this is not feasible, employ as "weak" a comparison group (i.e., with relatively low dosage of whatever is being studied) as is scientifically meaningful.

2. Employ those subjects who are most likely to profit from the experimental intervention.

3. Employ reliable dependent variables.

4. Employ dependent variables that are extremely sensitive to change.

5. Employ outcome variables that are directly (as opposed to indirectly) related to the experimental intervention.

6. Employ research designs that permit the statistical control of extraneous variables. These include the use of covariates, within-subject variables, and factorial designs.

7. Always conduct a power analysis to ascertain how many subjects must be employed to allow at least an 80% chance of rejecting the null hypothesis.

8. Employ as many subjects as economically and practically feasible. When one group is more expensive or difficult to run than another, consider randomly assigning more subjects to the latter.

Suggested Readings

By far and away the best book on designing experiments capable of achieving statistical significance is:

Lipsey, M. W. (1990). *Design sensitivity: Statistical power for experimental research.* Newbury Park, CA: Sage.
> This is not only an excellent and readable text on statistical power but a very good research methodology book. The author deals with all the elements relevant to designing sensitive experiments and, in my opinion, his book should be required reading for anyone contemplating a career in experimental research.

I would also recommend either of the following books to those conducting a power analysis:

Cohen, J. (1977). *Statistical power analysis for the behavioral sciences.* New York: Academic Press. (Reprinted 1988 and currently available from Lawrence Erlbaum.)
    This is the classic in its field. Besides giving a thorough general discussion of the concept and meaning of power itself, this book provides tables for ascertaining both power and the sample sizes needed for most common research designs.

Kraemer, H. C., & Thiemann, S. (1987). *How many subjects?* Newbury Park, CA: Sage.
    This book is perhaps a little easier to use than Cohen (1988), but it generally covers the same content.

There are a number of power analysis PC programs, the most popular of which is probably:

Borenstein, M., & Cohen, J. (1988). *Statistical power analysis: A computer program.* Hillsdale, NJ: Lawrence Erlbaum.

7

Conducting the Pilot Study(ies)

If you followed the preceding 29 rules conscientiously, you should be in possession of a very promising blueprint. Unfortunately, this is all you will have until a considerable amount of pilot work has been done to refine your intervention and outcome variables. Good experiments do not spring fully developed from the drawing board or a brainstorming session. All of their components must be grounded in theory, previous research, or extensive clinical experience. It is equally important that they all require a certain amount of developmental work before they can be successfully implemented, which operationally translates to Principle 30:

▼

Principle 30: **Always conduct at least one pilot study.**

▼

This is a rule that almost all researchers know but far too many ignore. In studies employing experimental interventions, however, it is especially essential for researchers to conduct their interventions with a limited number of subjects ahead of time, to ensure both their feasibility and the appropriateness of the various components that make them up.

The actual issues that need to be addressed via any given pilot study depend upon the nature of the specific study being planned. They are also dependent upon the researcher's degree of experience. Someone conducting a follow-up study employing only a minor design variation, for example, obviously will not need as much developmental work as someone about to attempt his or her first study in a given area.

Assuming the latter scenario, your pilot work will need to address each of the following questions:

1. How likely is the intervention to affect the outcome variable?
2. How responsive is the outcome variable likely to be?
3. How feasible are the experimental procedures in general?

Developing the Intervention

To expect to develop and test an intervention with no theoretical rationale or preliminary pilot work is analogous to a pharmaceutical company mixing some promising chemicals together and then administering the resulting concoction to AIDS patients in order to see if it will cure their disease. It just isn't reasonable to waste resources, either material or human, in such a fashion.

Even the most conceptually uncomplicated of studies, such as one assessing the effects of increasing the length of instructional class periods, requires either a sound theoretical rationale or a sound empirical rationale. (This might emanate from time-on-task theory or even a large-scale correlational study in which one of the correlates of learning was found to be the amount of instruction received; but to choose a variable with no such rationale would almost surely result in wasted effort.)

Simply recognizing what our independent (length of instruction) and dependent (achievement) variables were going to be, however, would still leave us a long way from developing a successful intervention. We would still need to make a number of decisions, a sample of which follows:

1. What grade level should we employ (e.g., college or elementary school children)?
2. What type of schools (e.g., public versus private) or students (e.g., average or special) will we employ?
3. What type of achievement (e.g., mathematical versus reading) and what type of learning (e.g., recall of facts versus understanding of concepts) will we measure?

4. What subject matter will be taught (e.g., operations involving fractions versus the use of algorithms for dealing with whole numbers)?

5. How long should the instructional interval be (e.g., an entire year versus a week)?

6. How long should the actual class periods be (e.g., 60 versus 45 minutes, or 40 versus 20 minutes)?

7. What type of teacher should we employ (e.g., experienced classroom teachers or research assistants whose actions are more under the investigator's control)?

Every intervention will have its own unique list of questions that need to be answered. Fortunately, the decisions that they reflect can always be guided by four basic criteria. In order of importance, these are:

1. Theoretical and clinical indicators. Every discipline has a unique body of knowledge that must be used to guide its research. This fact is the primary motivator for Principles 6 to 9. Using the class length example, if special education students were known or hypothesized to have relatively short attention spans, then they would probably not be good candidates for an intervention involving long class periods. If certain subject areas took longer than others to master, then the researcher might choose to avoid these in order to demonstrate as large a learning effect as possible as quickly as possible.

2. The researcher's personal objective for doing the study in the first place (Principle 14). If a researcher wished to influence public school policy, for example, this would mandate a number of the above decisions in and of itself. The experimental procedures would need to be made as veridical as possible, for example, to match actual everyday practices, and the intervention would need to be both practical and economically feasible. Thus, to facilitate its implementation, our educational researcher would want to employ class lengths that could be practically instituted (e.g., few schools would be likely to devote more than 120 minutes or less than 30 minutes to instruction in a single topic, regardless of the study's final outcome). If the researcher's interest were more of a basic and less of an applied bent, on the other hand, then he or she would not be constrained by as many practical constraints and could (within reason) define the intervention primarily to maximize its effect upon the outcome variable.

3. The likelihood of achieving the largest outcome differences possible.
Chapter 6 has already been devoted to this issue, but it is worth repeating
that your primary methodological objective as a researcher is to demonstrate that the intervention can result in salutary changes with respect
to the outcome variable(s). This means that, consonant with the first two
considerations above, you should always attempt to maximize your
effect size by every legitimate means. Thus, decisions regarding, say,
the experimental interval should be based upon how long it will take
the intervention to manifest itself. Similar considerations should affect
choices regarding the experimental curriculum, the actual instrument
chosen to measure the outcome variable, and so forth.

4. Practical considerations. Researchers must often do their studies
based upon available samples, constraints placed upon them by cooperat-
ing clinical agencies, and what can reasonably be asked of their subjects. Sometimes practical considerations such as these conflict with
one or more of the criteria mentioned above, in which case a decision
must be made as to whether the planned study is worth running under
the conditions offered. More often, however, it is necessary to modify
one's intervention to fit one's clinical constraints. The skill with which
the resulting trade-offs are made can, to a large extent, dictate the
ultimate utility of the resulting product.

   Although the above criteria are helpful in making the types of decisions
we are discussing here, they are certainly not sufficient in and of themselves. More often than not the researcher will not know, for example,
how long it will take for a particular intervention to manifest itself, and
to make such a determination on the basis of a guess (or intuition) is a
blueprint for disaster.
   What researchers must typically do, therefore, is try out different
theoretically/empirically justifiable variations of their interventions on
small groups of subjects until they find one that (a) can be practically
implemented, (b) does appear to be capable of maximally influencing
the specific outcome measure being employed, and (c) meets both their
personal and scientific objectives for conducting the study in the first
place.
   Although it is a hard truth for beginning researchers to accept, it is
an unfortunate fact of life that this preliminary developmental work
often takes more time and more effort than the final evaluation of the

intervention itself. The bottom line is, however, that insufficiently developed interventions just plain do not work.

As far as the intervention is concerned, the primary purpose of both this developmental work and a pilot study is to help provide answers to the following five questions. (If five unequivocal "yes" answers cannot be supplied to these questions, then you should either pick another intervention or do more pilot work.)

1. Do you have a sound theoretical or empirical rationale for the intervention as you have defined it? Such a rationale could consist of data collected from a pilot study that, say, demonstrates a pre-post outcome change in subjects exposed to the intervention. Alternately, previous research can serve here as well, although this would not preclude the necessity of conducting a pilot study to serve some of the other purposes detailed below.

2. Can you justify each component of the intervention in this manner? Many of the examples used in this book were purposefully chosen for their conceptual and procedural simplicity. For more complex socio-behavioral interventions, each separate component thereof should ideally be subjected to the same theoretical and empirical scrutiny.

3. Do you have good reason to believe that your intervention will indeed work? It is optimal that this belief should be based upon at least a preliminary trend or an effect generated by your pilot work.

4. Can the intervention be implemented, given the resources available to you? If your initial pilot work indicates that major procedural changes are necessary, then you should either do more pilot work or seek another environment in which to do your study.

5. Assuming you think your fine-tuned intervention will work, will it meet your personal and scientific objectives? A researcher who conducts the type of careful, thorough preliminary work that I am suggesting here seldom winds up with the same intervention he or she started out with. Some procedures must usually be altered slightly, while others must be added or dropped. Therefore, once you have arrived at a final definition of the intervention you plan to evaluate, I think it is a good idea to sit down and decide if your revised study will meet your objectives for doing the study in the first place (i.e., Principle 14). You might decide, for example, that the revised intervention is so complex that it could never be implemented in a real-life clinical setting. Or alternately, it might be so close to another intervention already tested that the study may not seem worth doing.

If you can answer the above questions affirmatively, however, it undoubtedly means that you have done the requisite developmental work to justify your intervention. It also means that you will already have a pretty good idea what your final results will be (assuming that you design the study following the advice tendered in the last few chapters), which, incidentally, is one of the primary purposes of conducting a pilot study. Regardless of folklore, *real-life scientists do not like surprises*. They like to know how a study is going to turn out before they conduct it—and ultimately so do their funding agencies.

Refining the Outcome Measure

Designing an experiment is like choreographing an intricate mating dance between the intervention and the outcome variable. These two entities have to be perfectly matched, or the researcher will have little or no chance of obtaining statistically significant results.

We have already talked a great deal about selecting an important, meaningful outcome variable. At this point, however, your task is to ensure that the manner in which you will actually measure this variable is optimal for the purposes at hand. The primary criterion for making this judgment resides in the implementation of Principle 25 (always employ outcome measures that are both reliable and sensitive to change).

The best way to do this is to conduct a pilot study in which you pretest a group of subjects with your proposed outcome measure, administer the intervention, and then posttest the same subjects with the same measure. If you cannot demonstrate a reasonably large numerical pretest/posttest gain, then your outcome measure may not be sensitive enough for the purposes at hand. It is not enough to demonstrate that your measure is highly reliable. Reliability does not guarantee sensitivity to change.

I would therefore suggest that, as one goal of your pilot work, you plan to ensure positive answers to the following four questions:

1. Is your proposed outcome measure reliable? Even though reliability per se is not the primary criterion for ensuring sensitivity, it is often (although not always) a necessary condition thereof. The internal consistency of a multi-item measure can also be obtained relatively easily by administering it to a single sample of subjects, hence this particular information is more likely to be obtainable from previous research.

2. Is the proposed variable sensitive to change or, more specifically, will it be responsive to the intervention? Again, a gross answer to this crucial question is usually best obtained by measuring a relatively few subjects before and after the experimental manipulation. The previous research literature can be helpful in this regard, but it is seldom definitive enough to preclude the necessity of an actual pilot study.

3. How much is the outcome variable likely to change over the proposed course of the study? This is really synonymous with estimating what the study's effect size is likely to be. It is dependent upon both the sensitivity of the outcome variable and the strength of the intervention; hence, one of the primary purposes of a pilot study is often to determine how long the subjects should be exposed to the intervention in question in order to demonstrate an optimal effect. This can be a crucial question, since its answer has a direct impact upon both the procedural and economic feasibility of the proposed study itself. (Answering this question sometimes necessitates administering the outcome measure more than twice during the course of a pilot study. In other words, if a sufficient change has not occurred at the first posttest, then the intervention would have to be extended and the pilot subjects tested repeatedly until something approaching a reasonable effect size is obtained.)

4. Can any preexisting measures (i.e., covariates) be identified that are correlated with the proposed outcome variable(s)? Effective covariates can often be identified from the previous research literature, but actual correlations can also be run on one's pilot data between potential co-variates and the outcome variables if 15 to 20 subjects are available. Similarly, pretest/posttest correlations can be obtained for the outcome measure itself to indicate the utility of using baseline values thereof as the covariate.

Ensuring the Feasibility of the Proposed Design

Even if you were able to start out with perfectly refined intervention and outcome measures, you would still not be assured that your design could be practically implemented in your targeted setting. It is almost always necessary to conduct a dry run of the entire intervention (and sometimes the control itself) with at least a few subjects, just to make sure that there are not some procedural glitches you haven't thought of.

Ironically, it is only inexperienced researchers who must be convinced of this necessity. Almost all experienced investigators have made enough mistakes that they take this step through simple self-defense. Once, as a graduate student, I personally hatched a brilliant plot for increasing the amount students could learn from studying a prose passage for a fixed period of time. It seemed extremely wasteful to me for them to reread parts of a passage that they had already learned. I therefore reasoned that if they were to delete what they had learned as they went, using a Magic Marker, then their study time would be more focused than that of students who did not have access to this intervention. Naturally, I didn't bother to conduct a pilot test of something this procedurally simple, hence I was shocked when I first heard the deafening sound of 30 Magic Markers being run across 30 papers at the same time. (Nor was I prepared for the noxious fumes emanating therefrom.) Needless to say, this particular study didn't wind up revolutionizing the way students studied.

With this example in mind, I would suggest that you pilot your experimental procedures with an eye toward providing positive answers to the following questions:

1. Can the experimental treatments be run as planned? In other words, are there unforeseen problems emanating from the intervention, the setting in which it is to be implemented, or some interaction between the two?

2. Can the treatments be monitored properly? For example, can you ensure that both the intervention and the control groups are behaving in the manner required of them? Can you be sure that cross-contamination (or one of the other artifacts discussed in Chapter 5) is not occurring?

3. Will subjects show up, sit through, and in general cooperate with the experimental protocol? Sometimes researchers simply expect too much of subjects, given the day-to-day constraints under which they operate. Sometimes our interventions are simply too onerous.

4. Will subjects complete the experimental protocol? This is especially important to determine for studies in which subjects must attend more than one experimental session. I have seen otherwise well-designed studies completely fall apart because of subjects showing up for only the first couple of sessions and not even being available for the final administration of the outcome variable. (In general it is always wise to require as little of your subjects as possible.)

5. Do subjects need to be paid to participate, and if so, how much? This can be an antidote for problems encountered in 3 and 4.

6. Are the experimental procedures unduly obtrusive? This may be ascertained by simply questioning the subjects after they have completed the pilot study requirements.

7. What types of subjects are most likely to profit from the experimental procedures? This is sometimes hard to ascertain within the limited confines of a pilot study, but often the administration of the instrument designed to measure the outcome variable can identify groups of subjects who score near its ceiling and hence cannot be expected to profit from the intervention, no matter how effective it otherwise might be.

Running Pilot Studies

It is hoped that all of the questions presented in this chapter will seldom need to be answered in any single pilot study. There is certainly nothing wrong with trying to avoid as much work in this regard as possible, such as by consulting with a colleague who has conducted a program of similar research in the area in which you are interested. (Even if you had to pay a consultant $200 or $300 out-of-pocket for a half-day of his or her time, you would still come out ahead in the long run. Alternately, you could try to enlist the consultant as a collaborator.) The published research literature can also be helpful in certain instances; but in the final analysis, I do not think the experiment exists that does not require some pilot work, and this is especially true with respect to administering the intervention(s) under conditions comparable to those you will encounter in the full-blown experiment.

There are really no hard-and-fast rules for running pilot studies, other than:

1. to be as systematic as possible,
2. to keep good records,
3. to conduct as many pilot studies as necessary to ensure that you have at least tentative answers to all of the above questions, and
4. to always run through your intervention with at least a few subjects, to make sure both that it is feasible and that your outcome variable is sensitive to change.

The number of subjects you need to employ in a pilot study depends to a certain extent upon the types of decisions that need to be made. If the reliability of the proposed outcome variable is an issue, for example, then a minimum of 15 to 20 subjects are probably needed. If a suitable target population needs to be identified, even more subjects may be required. If, on the other hand, these two parameters are already determined, and the researcher only needs to run through the experimental procedures in order to detect any unsuspected problems, as few as 5 or 6 subjects may be sufficient. There is also nothing wrong with conducting more than one (possibly simultaneously) pilot study to accomplish disparate purposes. Fifteen or 20 subjects, for example, could be employed to assess the psychometric properties of the outcome variable, while only 5 of these (or 5 completely different subjects) might be exposed to the intervention.

Regardless of the care with which you conduct your pilot work, however, you will almost always go into your final study with a few incompletely answered questions. What I have attempted to do in this chapter is show you how to reduce the number of question marks as much as possible via the conduct of thorough, careful pilot work. It is optimal that this would entail running through your entire experimental procedure (i.e., randomly assigning subjects to intervention and control groups and then actually implementing the entire experimental protocol). In the presence of limited resources, however, it is necessary to make compromises, such as the above-mentioned strategy of pretesting all available subjects, exposing them to the intervention, and posttesting them.

So although there may be no real rules concerning the best way to run a pilot study, you should always keep in mind that its ultimate purpose is to facilitate the successful running of the full-blown study. Further, since any results accruing therefrom will never be reported to the scientific literature, you should feel free to (a) change procedures in midstream, (b) try out different measuring instruments, and (c) in general violate any of the principles presented in this book in order to arrive at the one best way of accomplishing Principle 30. What you should not feel free to do is:

1. put too much credence in any observed numerical trends in your data unless actual experimental procedures (e.g., random assignment) are used, with as many as 8 to 10 subjects per group, or
2. plan to lump your pilot data in with the data actually obtained in the final study, even if your procedures remain the same (mainly because the possibility of doing this may unconsciously persuade you not to change a procedure that needs changing, based upon how the pilot results look). It is no time to get lazy, after all, when you are on the brink of conducting your first meaningful experiment.

Suggested Reading

This is an area about which not a great deal has been written. One exception includes:

Prescott, P. A., & Soeken, K. (1989). The potential uses of pilot work. *Nursing Research, 38,* 60-62.

8

Conducting the Actual Study

If you have refined your experimental blueprint to the point that you are relatively comfortable with the feasibility of your procedures and the appropriateness of your measures, it is time to begin a process that can be comparable to walking through a minefield: actually conducting the study itself. If there was ever any human activity to which Murphy's Law (i.e., "Anything that can go wrong will go wrong") applies, it is the conduct of an experiment. It is to that unfortunate fact that the following principle is addressed:

▼

Principle 31: **Always monitor the implementation of the experimental design with extreme care, to ensure its uniform implementation throughout the course of the study.**

▼

Sometimes it seems that the best-laid plans of researchers are more likely to go astray than are those of just about anyone else (with the possible exception of politicians). The most elegant of designs is worthless if it is not properly implemented. If we assume that a study's design is feasible to begin with, the most common reason for implementation failure comes from inadequate supervision on the part of the researcher.

In general, the more people involved in a study and the longer it runs, the more things there are that can go wrong.

What a researcher has to do, therefore, is be very compulsive about the details of his or her design and supervise its implementation very, very carefully. This is always easier if you are implementing the procedures yourself, but you will still have to monitor the research environment with extreme care, to ensure that you do not unconsciously allow your experimental protocol to change over time. (At an extreme level, it is not that uncommon for researchers attempting to evaluate the effectiveness of, say, a clinical treatment program to find that the intervention itself evolves and changes over the course of the study.)

The best way to ensure that these types of problems do not occur is to:

1. Write out a detailed, step-by-step description of the study design and the specific procedural steps to be taken. Begin with the inclusion/exclusion criteria for the subjects and proceed to the exact manner in which subjects will be assigned to groups, how they will be measured, and so on, through the entire process. This information will usually be available in the original proposal that is sent to the Institutional Review Board, but what I am suggesting here is an especially detailed, step-by-step listing of every component of the design, from identifying eligible subjects to administering the final posttest. (This list should also prove helpful in the search for experimental confounds, as suggested in Principle 18.)

2. Use this description to generate a study log in which all minute deviations from the planned protocol can be listed. This log should be conscientiously maintained throughout the course of the study. Its primary purpose, of course, is to prevent any such deviations from occurring in the first place or, at the very least, to prevent their recurrence.

3. Standardize every aspect of the design to the maximum degree possible. Write out scripts for the administration of both the intervention and the outcome and see that the exact wording of these scripts is adhered to over the course of the study.

4. If there is any subjectivity at all in the data collection process (e.g., if observations are employed as the outcome variable), train the individuals charged with this task rigorously prior to beginning the study, until an acceptable level of interrater reliability is obtained, and conduct unannounced spot checks thereof throughout the course of the study. (Previous research has indicated that interrater reliability is considerably higher when the observers know that they are going to be evaluated than when they do not.) If only one person is to be used to collect the data, employ another one during the pilot phase anyway to ensure that your data can be collected with a reasonable degree of interrater reliability.

5. Keep detailed, compulsive records on everything. Record all pertinent information on all subjects included in the study, for example, as well as those who refuse to participate or who drop out (including the reasons, if known). Record the dates of all experimental procedures. In short, record everything that occurs during the course of the study.

6. Regardless of your basic personality, be very aggressive during the conduct of your study to ensure that no preventable extraneous events interfere with your study protocol. You must always remember that your job is to run the cleanest possible study. This may be your best (and perhaps only) chance to make a contribution to the human condition. *Don't blow it.* I once ran a study in an elementary school in which the experimental protocol lasted only one hour. During the course of the study, the principal decided that it was time for his monthly fire drill and was absolutely adamant that he had to conduct it at this particular point in time, due to district regulations. Although generally a rather mild-mannered person, I was even more adamant and think I might have risked assault and battery charges if my colleague hadn't very kindly bowed to my concentrated whines and pleas.

Although conscientiously following these steps will go a long way toward ensuring the integrity of the final results, I think the following addendum to Principle 31 is necessary to maximize these benefits:

▼

Principle 32: **Delegate as little of the design implementation and monitoring aspects of the study as possible.**

▼

There are so many exceptions to this principle that I hesitate to give it the status of a hard-and-fast rule. I have, however, seen many very well conceived studies come to grief because their principal investigators seemed to feel that the more mundane aspects of running the study were somehow beneath their dignity to either perform or supervise. As stated earlier, I would personally never allow anyone (except perhaps a fellow research methodologist) to randomly assign my subjects for me. I would also never rely on clinical personnel (e.g., teachers, nurses, social workers) to collect my data for me. (Such professionals have other priorities and are simply not sufficiently trained to produce data of satisfactory quality to permit a precise test of a research hypothesis.) I would also not allow anyone to implement my experimental intervention whom I was not directly supervising or who did not have a direct stake in the study (e.g., a collaborator with whom I had had personal experience).

I realize that it is often necessary to devise some sort of sensible division of labor when it comes to running a particularly time-consuming research study. I would still counsel all serious researchers to be personally involved in the implementation process of their studies, to the maximum extent possible. When you cannot do something personally, I would suggest that you devise an extensive system of checks and balances in order to detect problems and inconsistencies as quickly as possible. The bottom line here is simply that:

> Running a research study requires both a great deal of skill and a great deal of commitment. Sometimes the only way to ensure that both of these attributes are present is to be there yourself.

Evaluating the Implementation of the Design

As soon as the final study data have been collected, I would counsel the researcher to sit down and carefully evaluate how well the protocol was implemented and the extent to which some of the things that could go wrong did. The presence of the detailed research log recommended above should help considerably in this process. In some cases, however, it is still a good idea to take the following additional precaution:

▼

Principle 33: **When feasible, actually survey your research subjects to obtain their perceptions of how the experimental protocol was implemented.**

▼

This survey can take any form you wish but should certainly concentrate on all suspected problems and weaknesses inherent in the design
genre employed. I have already mentioned my use of this technique to
document a suspicion that a control condition was too obtrusive, but
there are many other applications as well. It can be especially helpful,
for example, in documenting the extent to which the experimental protocol
was actually implemented or the degree to which between-group experimental contamination occurred.

Equipped with these results, plus those accruing from your procedural
log, I would next suggest that you compile a list of any errors or
shortcomings made during the course of your study, with an eye toward
evaluating their potential for producing both false positive and false
negative results. One way to do this is to write a detailed description of
your overall experimental procedures, honestly noting any errors. (Preferably, you should model this upon the type of journal article that you
plan to submit.) Next, you should attempt an honest appraisal of both
the probable and possible effects of these errors by providing a "yes"
or "no" response to Principle 34:

Principle 34: **After running your study and noting any procedural errors made, always ask yourself the following
question: Would the same results have accrued if these
errors had not been made?**

▼

It is probably a rare experiment in which no errors of any kind are
made. The purpose of evaluating the implementation of the experimental protocol, therefore, is to determine the probable impact of any
relatively minor errors that did occur. The fact that you have not yet
analyzed your data should facilitate your supplying an honest answer
to this sine qua non of all evaluative questions.

If the answer to the question embedded in Principle 34 is an unequivocal "no" (and this will be rare), I would suggest that you go back to the
drawing board and redo the study. (Any true scientist would prefer his
or her efforts to go unpublished than to have erroneous results printed
under his or her name.) Assuming that your study has been more or
less run as it was designed, however, it is now time for the most exciting

part of the research process: analyzing your data and finding out what your intervention has wrought.

Suggested Reading

There is very little written that I know of (other than this book) that will be much help to you in actually running your study. The best additional reading that I can give you at this point, then, is to read Chapter 8 again. The best additional advice I can give you is to be very careful.

9

Analyzing and Reporting the Results

Now comes the fun part. You have run your study and collected your data, so it is time to see if your intervention had its hypothesized effect. In other words, it is time to analyze your data.

This is definitely one part of the process that I would not delegate to anyone else. With the universal accessibility of easy-to-use statistical packages, you need absolutely no mathematical aptitude to be able to perform even the most complicated statistical analysis. Since the success or failure of your entire enterprise now rests upon your data being correctly analyzed, it seems ridiculous to me to turn this task over to a "statistician" and blindly hope that he or she performs it appropriately. Instead, I tender the following piece of advice:

Principle 35: **Take the time to learn to use one of the major statistical packages (i.e., SPSSx, BMDP, or SAS) so that you can personally analyze your own data.**

▼

The only reason I suggest using one of these packages is their availability. Of the three, SPSSx is probably the most commonly used in the social and behavioral sciences, although it has been my informal observation that SAS may be gaining on it. Ironically, BMDP and SAS produce more easily interpretable output for many of the types of analyses most commonly performed for experimental studies, but it doesn't really matter what you use as long as your program (a) includes factorial ANOVA/ANCOVA with a nesting option, (b) includes post hoc tests, and (c) permits data combination/transformation procedures.

How you learn to use the computer is, of course, your own business, although I personally recommend finding someone who is very conversant with the package of your choice and engaging him or her as a tutor. (Many academic computing centers routinely offer courses in the use of one or more of these packages as well, although I have never found these to be as helpful as a one-on-one tutorial.) Whether you use the mainframe or a PC is also up to you and the quality of the options your institution affords. In my experience, more and more researchers are opting for the flexibility of performing their analyses on their own PCs since the quality of their statistical software has improved dramatically over the past few years.

Regardless of the type of statistical package or the type of computer you finally decide upon, the most crucial part of the analytic process is undoubtedly data entry. There are two components to this phase: constructing a sensible coding scheme and entering the data accurately. Of the two, the second is more important as long as you understand that each variable must occupy a unique "column" in the data matrix and that all of the data you collect should be entered. (If you have a multiple-item measure that is used to generate one or more summated scores, for example, you should enter each subject's scores on each item and allow the computer to generate the actual scores to be used in the final analysis. Similarly, if you collect information on one or more variables for which you do not think you will have any use, enter it anyway. You may come back to your data in a year or so and be very happy that you have this particular piece of information available.)

Depending upon the size of the job, I don't always enter data into the computer myself, since people who do this for a living are faster and more accurate. *I always check its accuracy myself, however, because of my firm belief in the most commonly accepted truism in data analysis:* "Garbage In—Garbage Out." Although this may be one of the few research errors that I haven't personally been guilty of, I have seen so many different variations on this that I think it deserves the status of a principle:

▼

Principle 36: **Always check the accuracy with which your data have been coded and entered into the computer.**

▼

At the very least this entails:

1. Checking and rechecking your coding scheme. Some data can be most accurately entered directly from your records or the subjects' actual questionnaires. Sometimes it is best to code the data on 80-column forms especially made for this purpose; but regardless of the technique employed, you should always have the data proofread. (In other words, the original data, item-by-item and column-by-column, should be checked against what winds up in the computer.) When possible, the data entry process should also include verification, which basically entails entering it twice and manually checking any resulting discrepancies.

2. Performing a descriptive item-by-item run on the entered data, which includes a frequency distribution and summary statistics. This will allow you to ensure that your distributions look reasonable and that there are no data entered that are obviously outside the realm of possibility. (If Item #42, for example, is scored on a 5-point Likert scale and you find a "6," then something is obviously very wrong.)

Once you are confident regarding the accuracy of your data, you are ready to proceed with its statistical analysis. The first step in this process involves choosing an appropriate statistical procedure to test your primary hypothesis(es). This sometimes proves troublesome to beginning researchers but is really a relatively straightforward process in experimental studies: Unless you have chosen a highly skewed dichotomous variable as your experimental outcome, you will almost surely wind up using some form of analysis of variance (ANOVA) or analysis of covariance (ANCOVA).

The actual form this analysis takes will be dependent upon how you choose to implement Principle 27, but you should always choose your statistical procedure based upon the following principle:

▼

Principle 37: **Always include all of the sources of systematic variation (i.e., within-subjects/blocking variables and covariates) in your analytic scheme that you designed into your study.**

▼

The whole purpose of selecting such variables in the first place is to increase the statistical power available to you. The only way to cash in on this investment is to include these strategies in the statistical analysis itself.

Some beginning researchers have trouble identifying all of their sources of systematic variation, but I think answering the following series of questions will greatly facilitate this task, assuming that your data are not categorical in nature or do not possess an extremely skewed distribution. (Descriptors such as nominal, ordinal, interval, and ratio no longer have much meaning, but your outcome variable should be either continuous [i.e., a high number means that a subject has more/less of the attribute being measured than does a subject to whom a lower number is assigned] or dichotomous in nature [e.g., died/survived, passed/failed]. There are two schools of thought on this matter, but as with the advocates of the particle theory of light, the more conservative one is gradually dying out.)

To facilitate the selection of an appropriate analysis of variance/ covariance scheme, then, I offer the following set of questions:

1. Have you employed one or more variables strictly for control purposes? In other words, did you collect information on a preexisting variable specifically to use as a covariate? If you did, then you will be asking the computer to perform an analysis of covariance rather than an analysis of variance. You will also be reporting adjusted means rather than raw ones.

2. Did you match subjects or employ a crossover design, in which all subjects received both intervention and control conditions? If you did, you will instruct the computer that the intervention versus control contrast is a within-subjects or repeated-measures factor. You will also need to enter your data in such a way that the matched/identical subjects' data are contiguous.

3. Did you employ another independent variable besides the primary intervention versus control comparison or anything specifically designated as a covariate? In other words, do you have information on anything else that might mediate the effect of the intervention? Obviously, if you employed a between-subjects blocking variable (e.g., randomly assigned males and females separately to the intervention versus control groups), you will include gender as another "factor" in the analysis. Other potential independent variables may not be so obvious, such as when a study is performed at two different clinical sites (in which case these sites should be designated as a separate, two-group independent variable). Thus, if a researcher had conducted his or her two-group study in two different clinics, and employed baseline values of the outcome as a controlling variable, then the computer would be instructed to perform a 2 (intervention versus control) × 2 (Clinic #1 versus Clinic #2) analysis of covariance. If he or she had hypothesized that the intervention would be more or less effective for one gender than the other, then the analysis would be a 2 (intervention versus control) × 2 (Clinic #1 versus Clinic #2) × 2 (male versus female) analysis of covariance.

4. Was the outcome measure administered more than once? If it was administered twice, once as a pretest prior to the intervention and once as a posttest thereafter, I would counsel that the pretest be used as a covariate. If the outcome measure was administered more than once after the study began, however, you should probably employ another factor called "time" or "test administrations" and instruct the computer that this factor is a repeated measure. Thus if the 2 (intervention versus control) × 2 (Clinic #1 versus Clinic #2) × 2 (male versus female) design just mentioned had also employed a second administration of the outcome measure 6 months after the study was completed, to see whether the hypothesized effect for the intervention was transitory, then our researcher would instruct the computer to employ yet another two-group factor (immediate versus 6-month retention) and to represent it as a repeated measure. (Don't worry if this seems to be getting unduly complicated; the computer will do all the work for you.)

5. Was a nesting variable built into the design? If it was, don't forget to build this source of variation into the analysis as well.

6. Was more than one outcome measure employed? If so, you have one of two choices: You may employ a multivariate analysis of variance/ covariance (using the same model formed via answering questions 1 through 5, but simply telling the computer what your multiple dependent variables are) or you can perform an identical ANOVA/ANCOVA for each outcome measure employed. (Thus if all of the above alternatives applied, you would conduct a 2 × 2 × 2 × 2 repeated measures, nested multivariate analysis of covariance.) If you choose to conduct multiple univariate analyses, I would suggest that you consider adjusting your alpha level by dividing it by the number of contrasts involved. Thus, if you have four independent outcome variables, a conservative approach would be to use .0125 (.05/4) as your alpha level. Although most researchers do not do this, you should at least be aware that if you conduct enough statistical analyses, even using random numbers, you will get some results that are statistically significant by chance alone. (Actually, the use of a multivariate analysis of variance/covariance is a less conservative way of protecting your alpha level, although I prefer to use it only with outcome variables that are conceptually or empirically related to one another.)

Although this may seem a little involved, it is really quite straightforward since the answers to these six questions will point the way to the appropriate statistical analysis 99% of the time. Certainly there are always alternative ways to analyze any set of data or test any hypothesis, but this approach will result in the most commonly used procedures. (Anything that can be analyzed by an ANOVA/ANCOVA procedure, for example, can also be analyzed via multiple regression.)

Unfortunately, simply having the computer run an appropriate analysis of variance/covariance does not complete your data analytic tasks. I would suggest, therefore, that you keep the following strictures in mind:

1. You should not use your statistical analysis to decide when to end your study. Some researchers collect data only until they reach statistical significance. There is nothing at all wrong with this if they adjust their alpha levels based upon the number of "looks" at the data they plan to take. Thus, if your data are expensive or time-consuming to collect, you may want to plan to statistically analyze your results after you have run, say, half of the subjects your power analysis (Principle 28) indicates that you will probably need. This is fine as long as you protect your alpha level (which can be done by dividing it by the number of "looks" you plan to take).

2. Remember that your hypothesis(es) is stated in terms of a single contrast, so make sure that the final statistic you use to test it (them) reflects this single contrast. A sage senior statistician once criticized a very elegant and complicated analytic scheme that I had developed by stating that he had never been able to interpret any statistic that had "more than one degree of freedom." At the time I marveled at his parochialism, but I later understood that what he had said is really a cornerstone to applied statistical analysis itself. Thus, on the most simplistic level, he meant that if you have a three-group design (e.g., two intervention groups and a single control), the overall statistic (F ratio) that the computer will provide as a result of your one-way ANOVA or ANCOVA is pretty useless as far as interpreting your results. You must follow it up with some kind of post hoc procedure to see which groups differed from which other groups. The same is true of interactions and all other "higher level" effects. In the final analysis, it will be your group-by-group comparisons that you will use to decide whether your hypothesis has been supported. (This is one reason that I have advocated two-group designs: They produce overall and interactive contrasts that possess only one degree of freedom.)

3. Make sure that your data meet the assumptions required of your chosen statistical procedures. All statistical procedures require that some assumptions be met regarding variable distributions and/or relationships with one another. The additional readings suggested for this chapter treat all of these in considerable detail, but generally speaking you may need to adjust your alpha level (most texts dealing with ANOVA/ANCOVA will explain how to do this) a bit under the following conditions:

   a. For a factorial ANOVA not employing a repeated measure or a within-subject factor, if unequal numbers of subjects are contained in the various groups and their variances are significantly different from one another. (If only one of these conditions prevails, most researchers don't worry about it.) If the numbers of subjects are quite different among the groups, however, then you should probably interpret any interactions among your variables with caution.
   b. For an ANCOVA, if the covariate's correlation with the outcome variable is significantly different for your different groups. This

rarely occurs in true experiments but should be checked. Also, if a factorial ANCOVA is being employed, condition a, above, also holds.

c. For repeated measures and randomized block designs employing more than two groups for the within-subjects factor, when an assumption called *sphericity* is not met (which would indicate that the repeated measures correlated differently with one another across groups and their variances were different). This is routinely tested by most of the major statistical packages.

Although some people would disagree, I would argue that if these assumptions are met, then you should feel free to go ahead and interpret any statistically significant differences accruing from your analysis on face value.

4. In relation to 2, don't go on fishing expeditions to try to achieve statistical significance when your original analysis does not produce same. I strongly advocate the secondary analysis of data as well as the use of exploratory techniques. Searching for potential interacting or mediating variables for the express purpose of having something statistically significant to report, however, is never appropriate. If you have collected enough information on your subjects you can almost always find some subgroup that will behave differently from your sample as a whole. All too often researchers "pretend" that such a secondary finding was one of the main foci of their study to begin with. It has been my experience, however, that a posteriori *aptitude-by-treatment interactions* (as these findings are often called) seldom replicate, and few things are more injurious to a scientist's reputation than producing results that cannot be duplicated.

5. After you have tested your primary hypothesis(es), then you should conduct secondary and exploratory analyses on your data to see what else may be operating therein. Be on the lookout for relationships or effects that can serve as the basis for your next study. Make sure that your results are not unduly influenced by one or two outliers, and that they meet the prerequisite assumptions surrounding the statistical procedure you employed. See if certain types of individuals do seem to respond better (or worse) to your intervention than others. In other word , enjoy yourself. Just remember that anything you find here will have to be replicated before you can place a great deal of credence in it. Also, remember to report any such findings as secondary analyses and not pretend that it was a primary focus of the study to begin with. If you find anomalies in your data distributions, analyze them using more conservative statistical procedures, to ensure that your results are not artifactual. In other words, be careful, thorough, and creative.

Publishing the Results

If there is some question whether a tree falling unheard in a forest makes any sound, then it is definitely questionable whether unpublished research is science. Results that no one knows about certainly won't add to our cumulative knowledge or have the potential of helping anyone. Whether your intervention works or not, then, I offer the following commandment:

Principle 38: **Once you have analyzed your data, publish your results quickly.**

▼

In the process of conducting your study, you have expended scarce societal and scientific resources. This is true regardless of whether your research was formally funded; there is no such a thing as a free research study. (If nothing else, your subjects devoted time and effort to the enterprise, and that should not be squandered.)

Even if you did not achieve statistical significance, you should still attempt to publish your results so someone will be able to improve upon your procedures or at the very least not waste their time conducting the same study. Also, with the advent of meta-analysis it becomes increasingly important for all researchers to publish their results, so that these summative analyses (which can be extremely influential) are as accurate and exhaustive as possible. Finally, from a career perspective, you will never be considered a successful scientist if you do not publish. (Even if you wind up not being a scientist, published research on your résumé will prove helpful to you at some point or other in your career.)

I was personally guilty of violating Principle 38 early in my career and I now regret this. At one point I had so many opportunities to conduct research (and was so driven to do so) that I would often simply throw

away the results of an experiment that did not reach statistical significance and conduct another one. I still find conducting research to be
more fun than writing up the results, but the advent of word processors
has made this latter task much less onerous. Furthermore, if you follow
the sequence of principles presented in this book, your research report
will be practically written by the time your study is completed.

Your *literature review*, for example, will be completed, and the
abstracts you have written for each study will make this section relatively easy to complete. Your *methods* section will probably already be
written, since you have undoubtedly had to submit a proposal to your
Institutional Review Board. If not, then your research diary should make
this section extremely easy to write. The *results* section is the most
straightforward and least time-consuming of all to write, especially for
experimental research. This only leaves the *discussion* section, which
is really nothing more than a measured attempt to explain why you
obtained the results that you did and your assessment of where they fit
into the scientific literature. I would estimate, therefore, that you should
be able to write a good first draft of a scientific journal article in 2
uninterrupted 8-hour days—if you do so immediately after you have
completed your study. The longer you delay, the more imposing the task
is likely to appear and the less likely you are to complete it. (This is one
of the primary reasons why so few individuals ever get around to
publishing the results of their doctoral dissertation research.) Since
unpublished research really is little better than no research at all, *it is
therefore imperative that you do not postpone this final, crucial step.*

Although I will not delve deeply into the "how" of writing an exemplary
research report, or of getting the resulting manuscript accepted, I will
offer a few hints in this regard. First, however, I would like to frame all
of this advice in the form of a recycled principle, whose basic message
I hope has become familiar by now:

▼

Principle 39: **When publishing the results of your research,
be absolutely, uncompromisingly, unfashionably honest.**

▼

This means that if something went wrong in the conduct of your study,
admit it up front, when you present your procedures, and in closing, when
you discuss your results. Few experiments are run with no procedural

glitches. It is equally important that you do not fail to mention something that might have a bearing on the interpretation of your results because you are afraid that it will prejudice the acceptance of your paper. I realize that it is sometimes difficult to admit one's failings, but from a Machiavellian point of view, I think that it is often advantageous to do so. It can steal a reviewer's thunder to have the author admit something rather than allow him or her to "discover" it. We scientists also secretly value modesty in others (even if few of us ever indulge in this particular vice ourselves), so if someone admits freely that his or her study is not perfect (and does not attempt to oversell its importance), this can often prejudice reviewers in its favor.

Similarly, although perhaps not falling under the category of actual dishonesty, *do not play games when publishing your results*. Do not, for example, break your study into its absolutely "least publishable units" and try to get a dozen publications out of a single study. (It is far better to obtain one well-received, often-cited publication than multiple small ones tucked away in obscure sources that no one other than meta-analysts will ever read.) Obviously, you should not publish the same study in journals from different disciplines under different titles. You should not even publish your secondary analyses as a separate article, unless you are up-front about what you are doing and cite the primary study upon which it is based. You should not enter into publishing agreements with colleagues, whereby you list them as authors on your manuscripts if they reciprocate with theirs. In other words, *don't play games*. Be straightforward, be honest, and do not trivialize the hard work you have put into running your study in the first place.

With these disclaimers, then, I offer the following advice regarding getting your manuscript accepted for publication:

1. Choose the outlet that appears to publish the highest quality research in your area and specifically tailor your manuscript for it. In the course of your literature review, you will have learned the primary journals that publish the type of study that you have just completed. Get a copy of their submission specifications, read some recent articles to get a feel for the style of writing preferred, and prepare your manuscript accordingly. You should be somewhat realistic in your choice of journals and you may want to avoid those with extremely high rejection rates (hence, I wouldn't suggest that you automatically submit your first manuscript to *Science* or *The New England Journal of Medicine*). It doesn't hurt to aim high, however, and it also doesn't hurt that the results of competently run experiments are usually easier to publish than those of any other type of research.

2. Prepare the manuscript as professionally as possible. Use a high-quality laser printer and a good word-processing or desktop publishing program. Use a high-quality copier. The appearance of your manuscript, while not the primary factor, will have an impact upon its acceptance or rejection.

3. Always have at least one knowledgeable colleague proof your final manuscript. Request that your reviewers supply substantive and stylistic suggestions. Have them be on the lookout for areas that do not flow logically or in which you have supplied insufficient information. If you have access to a copy editor, by all means use one, even if you need to pay him or her.

4. Include all the information your audience needs to evaluate and replicate your study. Always report means and standard deviations, for example, and do not skimp on any relevant methodological details.

5. Do not exaggerate the importance of your study or its implications. It is natural for you to be enthusiastic about your own research, but excessive hype will turn your reviewers off. In science exaggeration is a form of dishonesty.

6. Submit your manuscript for publication and begin your next study immediately. You will find the process considerably easier the second time around, and the final product will probably be better science.

7. If revisions are requested once your manuscript is reviewed, make them promptly and resubmit the paper quickly. Few manuscripts are accepted without some changes requested, and it is a good idea to accede to your reviewers' requests, unless you think that the resulting changes will misrepresent your results (which is rare). It doesn't matter if you disagree with the reviewers and the editor at this point; the best strategy is to make the changes and indicate their location in your resubmission letter to the editor. It also doesn't hurt to thank the editor and his or her reviewers for their insightful comments, even if you secretly suspect that they are morons.

8. If your manuscript is rejected, immediately revise it (if you feel that some of the reviewers' objections were warranted) and submit it to the journal of your second choice. There is no shame in having a manuscript rejected. A very large proportion of such decisions is dependent upon who was chosen to review a particular manuscript (and perhaps even the mood they were in when they did so). It is crucial, therefore, that you be thick-skinned and resubmit your study as quickly as possible. If you are persistent you will eventually get your study accepted, and the resulting manuscript may even be superior, based upon the feedback you got along the way.

Regardless of the ultimate disposition of your manuscript, however, the important thing is to continue to do research. If it is warranted, do a follow-up study to extend what you have just discovered. If your just completed study seems to have led to a dead end, use this knowledge to begin formulating your next hypothesis. In other words:

▼

Principle 40: **Have your next study underway as soon as (and preferably before) you submit the results of your first one for publication.**

▼

If science really is a river of effort without end, you have at least gotten your feet wet, and perhaps the river is flowing just a little faster because of it. Even more important, perhaps the world will someday be a slightly better place because of your contribution and, to paraphrase Dr. Salk, perhaps "The ultimate reward for good work is the opportunity for our children to do more."

Suggested Readings

Given this book's emphasis upon experimental research, the most applicable statistical texts are those dealing with analysis of variance/covariance. To avoid dating myself, I will not recommend my dog-eared copy of Winer's *Statistical Principles in Experimental Design.* Instead, three of a great many useful current texts (in order of accessibility for the nonmathematically inclined) are:

Stevens, J. (1992). *Applied multivariate statistics for the social sciences* (2nd ed.). Hillsdale, NJ: Lawrence Erlbaum.

Keppel, G. (1991). *Design and analysis: A researcher's handbook* (3rd ed.). Englewood Cliffs, NJ: Prentice-Hall.

Maxwell, S. E., & Delaney, H. D. (1990). *Designing experiments and analyzing data: A model comparison perspective.* Belmont, CA: Wadsworth.

Computer Manuals

Choices of manuals for statistical programs are obviously dependent upon the statistical package you decide to use (or which are available for your use). The only piece of advice that I can provide here, therefore, is to actually purchase one, since you will ultimately need to own it.

Writing Aids

There are many, many books dedicated to helping their readers write better. Some are devoted to writing empirical papers, such as:

Day, R. A. (1979). *How to write and publish a scientific paper.* Philadelphia: ISI Press.

Some are general (but still helpful):

Strunk, W., & White, E. B. (1979). *The elements of style* (3rd ed.). New York: Macmillan.

Some are both and contain important information about specific scientific styles:

American Psychological Association. (1983). *Publication manual of the American psychological association.* Washington, DC: Author.

The Most Important Additional Reading of All

Once you decide to pursue a scientific career, it is essential that you monitor the journals in your field regularly. Most disciplines have a general research journal associated with their primary professional organization, as well as several more specialized vehicles that will routinely publish studies in your general area of interest. If you can afford it, subscribe to a couple of these, but in any case read them routinely as they come out. Also, remain literate with respect to the major scientific policy issues in general by keeping an eye out for articles in the newspaper as well as monitoring such periodicals as *The Chronicle of Higher Education* and *Science*.

Index

About the Author

Dr. R. Barker Bausell is currently Director of the Office of Research Methodology at the University of Maryland School of Nursing at Baltimore. His most recent book is *Advanced Research Methodology: An Annotated Guide to Sources* (Scarecrow Press, 1991). He has served as the editor-in-chief of *Evaluation and the Health Professions* for the past 17 years (and was one of its two founding editors). He has written more than 100 books, articles, and papers in the general areas of research methodology, preventive research, and educational research.

Dr. Bausell was awarded the Outstanding Research Award by the National Wellness Conference in both 1986 and 1987 and was also one of the first educational researchers ever to experimentally manipulate class size, teacher experience, and teacher knowledge. His current activities include the compilation of a directory of all existing meta-analyses and the development of a framework for evaluating health care reform.